THE PSYCHOLOGY OF MENTAL HEALTH

The Pursuit of Psychological Quality

C. FRANKLIN TRUAN

The Psychology of Mental Health: The Pursuit of Psychological Quality

Published by Wheatmark®
2030 East Speedway Boulevard, Suite 106
Tucson, Arizona 85719 USA
www.wheatmark.com

ISBN: 978-1-62787-842-5
ISBN: 978-1-62787-843-2
LCCN: 2020917807

Bulk ordering discounts are available through Wheatmark, Inc. For more information, email orders@wheatmark.com or call 1-888-934-0888.

My use of male gender pronouns is in no way meant to demean any other gender. It is standard or convention for ease of writing and reading. The material presented in this book applies equally to everyone.

Contents

Contents

Contents

Contents

Preface

Among the earth's living creatures, man is uniquely gifted with the exceptional abilities of conceptual thought, conscious self-awareness, propositional speech, and reasoned thinking. Man has used these gifts to become the dominant species of the earth. Intellectually, man functions at superior levels when compared to all other earthly creatures. His intellectual and technological accomplishments are astonishing.

At the same time man's accomplishments in the psychological domain pale in comparison. Psychologically, modern man has not significantly advanced from his cave-dwelling ancestors. His psychological thinking and behavior are predominately adolescent. He has accepted self-contradicting morality and original sin as his compass for right and wrong, and violates these simple standards every day. He lives in a psychological double bind that he has created.

Interpersonally, man chooses to be guided by self-serving flexible values that are destructive to him as an individual, to his own society, and among societies of the world. Because of the volitional choice to avoid learning and instead accept ignorance in the psychological domain, humans have all but assured continual strife within themselves, and mutual destruction among peoples. Man's inhumanity to man is leading us all toward self-destruction.

Collectively and individually, man has continually chosen to emphasize differences among people instead of seeing that we are all of equal value and seeking common ground. For his own individual or collective profit, he has used and abused his fellow man without regard for their rights or their welfare. Despite centuries of religious dogma demanding but a few constructive values, man has chosen hypocrisy as a valued hallmark while he claims otherwise. Although man professes valuing others, he continues to actually value only himself and his immediate desires over his own psychological welfare and the welfare of others. Valuing others is given only token status and token self-serving attention.

Man continues to choose money, power, and status over truth, justice, and equality. He has even chosen immediate self-gratification over preserving his environment. He has chosen to sacrifice the future of his progeny for present gain.

Man's future survival depends on him growing up psychologically. He must aspire to be the human being he is capable of becoming. He must cease being hypocritical by professing values that he does not actually live. Man must choose to value and live ethically and maturely instead of focusing on immediate self-indulgence and personal profit. *He must learn how to be mentally healthy in order to constructively affect the mental health of his offspring instead of passing along mental illness and psychological ineptitude to succeeding generations.*

For better or worse, mankind's future is always written by his decisions—the quality of his thinking. If human beings are to advance psychologically or even survive, it will be because *reality, reasoning, and psychological responsibility* have become the foremost lived values; man will have learned to really care for the welfare of all—not just himself and those who are like him.

The purpose of this book is to provide understanding and direction to man's greatest challenge—his own psychological health and its enhancement. That understanding must begin with identifying, learning, and actually living the physiognomies of mental health and interpersonal competence. Those characteristics and competencies must be taught as principles and skill-based behaviors. Prevention of mental illness and fulfillment of man's psychological potential are the goals.

Finally, this book is about what is possible and how to begin the transformation process toward these goals. It's time to take responsibility for who we are as a society and as individuals, and who we are not. It's time we held ourselves accountable for what we can be. The mental health and mental welfare of both ourselves and our progeny depends on all of us making a commitment to achieving the goal of living psychological quality.

Acknowledgments

Before I present my ideas concerning mental health, which I have developed in over fifty years of experience in the field, I would like to acknowledge a few individuals from the fields of psychology and philosophy and from my personal life who have made significant contributions to the formation of both my philosophical and pragmatic positions regarding mental health.

These individuals have something in common that separates them from most people: psychological independence from their respective culture and the internal motivation and courage to challenge accepted norms and unsound beliefs of their time. These individuals were full-fledged members of their respective societies, at least on the surface, yet sought constructive change for all mankind. In each case, their quest for truth was enabled and guided by their capacity for objective, reasoned thinking.

I will begin by acknowledging three prominent historical figures who most of us have been introduced to: Benjamin Franklin, Thomas Jefferson, and Franklin Delano Roosevelt. I have singled them out for one reason. They were politicians, but they were also statesmen. As statesmen they stood for what was right and good for the nation instead of what was advantageous for themselves as individuals. In addition to being statesmen, they stand out as original and independent thinkers who also contributed to society as scientists, inventors, and authors. Above all, their commonly held principle was *the pursuit of practical and beneficial truth guided by reality and reasoned thinking.*

In more recent times, and in a different arena, I would like to acknowledge several philosophy and psychology professionals who have greatly contributed to my professional education by helping me establish a clearer vision of mental illness and mental health. As independent and original thinkers, they focused on providing an accurate picture of human thought and behavior and sought to give clarity and understanding to the psychological experience of human existence. Their work exemplifies original insight guided by the pursuit of objective reality and functional subjective truth. Additionally, they all championed the principle of reasoning-based thinking being the only method by which man has for discerning subjective truth. Finally, they all had the courage it takes to stand up to conventional wisdom.

Bertrand Russell, Ayn Rand, Nathaniel Branden, Carl Rogers, and Robert R. Carkhuff are but a few of the individuals whose works have made significant and lasting impressions on me and my efforts as a psychologist, philosopher, and author. Other significant contributors to my educational enlightenment represent a variety of psychological schools of thought. These include self-psychology theorists Heinz Kohut and L. Guy Chelton; psychoanalytic phenomenologists George E. Atwood and Robert D. Stolorow; and cognitive psychology theorists, including Albert Ellis, William Glasser, and Vittorio Guidano.

Finally, I would like to acknowledge those who have probably taught me the most over the past fifty years: the many patients I have encountered in clinical practice and the countless numbers of students I have had the pleasure of teaching.

Introduction

The most critical factor in the development and maintenance of mental health is the foundational and sustained quality of the individual's self-concept—what the individual has learned to believe as truth about himself as a person.

My career in the field of mental health began in the mid-1960s. Upon returning from active military service in the U.S. Army, I spent a year doing volunteer counseling at Quaker House in Atlanta, Georgia, helping young men make decisions that would affect the course and quality of their lives. It was 1967, and there was a growing tide of resistance to our involvement in Vietnam.

I spent the next few years working at the Centers for Disease Control (CDC) while pursuing an undergraduate degree. In addition to my full-time job, I did volunteer work in counseling with both the CDC as an Equal Employment Opportunity counselor, and at the Bridge for Runaways, a community counseling center devoted to helping runaway teens reunite with their families. It was at the Bridge that I actually witnessed clinical counseling being conducted by professionals with degrees in mental health. I was in awe and mystified by the skills some of the counselors displayed. I was hooked. I became an enthusiastic student of verbal and nonverbal counseling skills and interpersonal processes in general.

I graduated with a BS in social psychology and urban life from

Georgia State University while working full-time and going to school at night. My classes taught me little about clinical psychology, but my motivation was not dampened. I began looking elsewhere for answers. My volunteer experiences and the fact that I now possessed a college degree made it possible for me to seek a paid position in counseling for the first time. I was able to obtain employment at the Fulton County Juvenile Court in Atlanta as a probation officer/counselor. Unfortunately, the counseling part of the job was nonexistent, and I would be limited to giving the probationer the rules for their behavior and threatening dire consequences should there be any infractions.

My vocational goal was to be a counselor, not a policeman. In order to pursue this goal in such a restricted setting, I divided my caseload into two groups: adolescents who actually wanted help and those who were not willing or able to see that they needed help. With an overwhelming caseload of eighty to ninety offenders, I found less than half really wanted my help. Once I had identified the adolescents who wanted help, my next goal was to involve their families in the counseling process. It was apparent that incarceration or being put on probation was not helping these adolescents. The recidivism rate for identified miscreants at that time was 80 percent. I also noted that if by some miracle a stint in the youth detention center was able to actually help any of the adolescents, they would return to making the same mistakes once they were back in their dysfunctional families. I also observed that quite often the delinquent adolescent's role in the family system was that of identified patient or scapegoat. In dysfunctional families it is often the strongest child who carries the burden of being the sick or bad member, thereby letting the others feign being normal. It seemed like a no-brainer to involve as much of the family as possible in the counseling process while the adolescent was on probation.

My efforts were rewarded after a few months when the two juvenile court judges there saw the progress I was making with families. They encouraged and supported my efforts to involve families in the rehabilitation effort. I felt like I was on the right track. I was pursuing my goal of becoming an effective helper and had identified a patient population who truly needed help. The judges made it possible for me to start the first integrated program within the juvenile court system, which blended family counseling with traditional probation services.

My family counseling program did well for several months and was making a difference in the lives of the adolescents and families that participated in the program. However, after about a year, I was notified by my superiors that the program would not continue. Apparently, the senior staff were against changing the traditional probation orientation. They were used to being police officers of the court, not counselors. My program was a threat, and politics prevailed.

I had already begun thinking about going to graduate school, and the closing of my program at the juvenile court made my decision final. With a graduate degree in counseling, I would be moving in the right direction toward my new goal of vocational independence. Additionally, there was another major reason that I needed to go back to school: I needed to learn more in-depth knowledge about psychology. I felt my clinical skills were above average, but I was not satisfied. I knew there was much I did not know. While working at the juvenile court, I had often been asked how I was able to talk to difficult adolescents and get them to open up. I was not able to answer the question. They wanted to know, but so did I, and graduate school was where I was going to find answers.

I reasoned that if I could understand the underlying secrets that enabled my counseling effectiveness, I would be able to use that conscious knowledge to improve my skills. Additionally, I would be able to teach those skills to others. I would spend the next six years at GSU earning two graduate degrees: a master's degree in counseling and a PhD in counseling psychology.

During those years in graduate school, I was successful in learning the process skills of any good counselor. I was able to compare my skill level with others more advanced. By my second year, I was teaching counselor skills in my department as a graduate teaching assistant. Teaching became my preferred mode of learning.

For me, achieving goals has always opened doors to allow me to see and set more goals for myself. My interest now shifted from counselor skills to other factors that contributed to clinical effectiveness. My doctoral dissertation was a research project that attempted to isolate personal characteristics and demographic variables such as age and the amount of previous helping experience. The goal of my study was to isolate the characteristics that predict counselor clinical effectiveness. With this predictive knowledge, the university could grant entrance to individuals more likely to become clinically effective in the field of counseling. At a minimum the bottom 20 percent could be redirected toward pursuing degrees that did not require higher levels of clinical skill. My work was successful and positively received. However, in private I was told that clinical skills were deemphasized, if considered at all, because funding was based on filling seats in the program. Therefore, the requirements for entrance were primarily intellectual. Clinical competence was left to chance.

I completed my degrees in 1978 and began a two-year internship that would make me eligible to become licensed as a psychologist. I began my private practice as a psychologist in 1984. However, I was still not satisfied with my attained level of knowledge or skills. Intellectually I had learned about various theoretical approaches, the symptoms of many different pathologies, and countless possible treatment methods, but I knew I still had much to learn. The various theories and methods I had studied all seemed to conflict with each other, and their methods seemed only partially effective at best.

I knew my clinical skills would continue to improve through focused experience. Therefore, my focus now turned logically to knowledge and answers at the theoretical level. Specifically, I wanted a broad theory that would explain the nature and causes of mental illness to my satisfaction. For example, I felt that I knew very little about addiction and its true cause. I had also observed that too many people seemed dissatisfied with themselves but did not know why.

I also wanted more knowledge about the origins and elements of mental health. I was not satisfied with the traditional system, which focused primarily on pathology. The emphasis was on diagnosing pathological behavior and then concentrating on symptom reduction. In order to believe in what I was doing as a professional, I wanted to have clear goals for treatment and understand the pro-

4

cesses that would achieve them. I also needed to know more about what constitutes mental health. Successful treatment must have a clear goal. Broadly, that goal is mental health. Therefore, the ability to lead someone toward the goal of mental health means that the helper *must know what mental health is and how to get there.*

I began my private practice as both teacher and learner. I helped others while I searched for answers. In 1987 I had an opportunity to do a yearlong internship at a groundbreaking clinical treatment center known as F.A.C.E., which specialized in the treatment of eating disorders. During that internship, my supervisor and founder of the center, Dr. L. Guy Chelton, introduced me to the theories and treatment methodologies of self psychology. It was there that I learned about the power of a person's beliefs about himself in determining the course in quality of life. With this new knowledge about the significance of self-concept in determining mental illness and mental health, I returned to my private practice.

During my years in private practice, I have worked with many clients from diverse backgrounds with a great variety of specific psychological and interpersonal problems. Common to all, however, was *the need to improve the quality of their inner relationship with themselves and the quality of their relationships with family, friends, and the community.* As my career progressed, I began to see important common and dominant themes in the issues presented by clients. The themes present in most people were

- the acceptance of irrational and destructive concepts as truth, especially beliefs about themselves;

- the presence of illogical non-reasoned thinking processes and a corresponding lack of faith in the efficacy of their own minds; and

- the absence of knowledge or awareness of the importance of constructive and sustained psychological growth as part of their lives.

I then began to generalize these themes beyond the immediate issues of clients to everyone seeking to improve the *psychological quality* of their lives. Simply stated, people desiring mental health and psychological quality in life must seek to live in reality and learn to identify reasoned based truth. They must learn and incorporate reasoned thinking with objective reality to understand themselves and to be functional in the world. They would also see this as a lifelong endeavor, a way of living, the continuous act of becoming. It is only through valuing and living these psychological principles that they can find the quality they seek.

I wanted to know more about the level of awareness of these themes and about people's knowledge of psychology and mental health. How do people view their own mental health? Do they value their mental health and psychological growth? What is the general perception and state of knowledge about mental health and mental illness? More specifically, how aware is the general public about the quality of their psychological health and interpersonal functioning? Are there standards of mental health, such as healthful principles and values and competencies that enable personal assessment and provide developmental direction for people to set and achieve higher levels of psychological quality? What is the overall state of psychological knowledge in society?

Representative Perceptions about Psychology, Mental Illness, and Mental Health

The domain of psychology remains a mystery, or an enigma, and something to be avoided by most people. Mental illness and mental health are topics most people know little about and prefer not to broach unless it's a quick attempt to be humorous. In fact, just thinking about mental illness can evoke anxiety. Mental health and illness are feared because they are the unknown.

As a consequence of both fear and ignorance, the quality of everyone's mental health has historically been left to chance. Leaving mental health to chance has created fertile ground for the ever-increasing growth of mental illness and the continued failure of mankind to grow psychologically to its full potential for maturity, morality, ethics, and even peace among peoples of the world.

The negative effects of this irresponsible attitude toward the psychological domain are observed and felt by all of us every day. From psychological problems in one individual or in a family to the social ills of our nation and the world, we reap the destructive results of ignoring and remaining ignorant of our own psychology.

We lack preventive psychological education for children and adults, and our treatment methods have failed to stem the tide of mental illness. Mass shootings, hate crimes, suicides, meaningless wars, homelessness, failed marriages, child abuse, and even poor parenting are everyday examples of problems that stem from mental illness, social disadvantage, destructive values, and interpersonal deficits of individuals and societies.

The general reaction to these tragedies is to wonder why and to pray for the victims and the survivors. Mental illness, be it clinical or subclinical, the factor most wrongdoers have in common, is either overlooked or given a token mention as a possibility. That which people do not understand remains a mystery to be denied and feared. The major reason people do not recognize or address the real issue is that psychological understanding is limited by the perceiver's attained levels of psychological health and knowledge. And furthermore, people can only perceive and solve problems *at the level they understand them. They cannot see beyond the level of their own psychological functioning.*

Out of ignorance and fear, as individuals and as a society, we choose to ignore the obvious: mental illness adversely affects us all. At any time, in any society, millions of individuals are consciously having to deal with mental illness issues. At the same moment, millions of others who are also afflicted, either clinically or sub-clinically, remain in abject ignorance and without treatment.

To address the ever-increasing problems of modern society, we must begin with the growing tide of mental illness. Society's role in contributing to mental illness must be addressed with real solutions instead of token gestures aimed at placating dissenters so real change can be avoided. Real solutions must also include educating the public about the familial causes of mental illness. Mental illnesses that are passed from generation to generation can be stopped if people know more about their causes and have direction for change and prevention. People also have a right to know what mental health is and how to acquire it and teach it to their progeny. Psychology should not remain a mystery or the feared unknown.

Just as most people assume they are going to heaven when they die, most also choose to assume they are mentally healthy. However, the facts state that at any given time, one in five people are suffering some type of mental illness. In the United States, that means that 20 percent of the population is currently dealing with mental illness. With a population of 320 million, that means that 60 million are afflicted at any given time. That 20 percent number represents only those who are identified as having mental health problems. Millions of others remain undiagnosed and suffer subclinically in dysfunctional families or alone in isolation.

Mental illness is pervasive in all societies. It is not restricted to a particular class, race, or socioeconomic group. *It is truly a pandemic.* For an individual, if ignored or denied, mental dysfunction will worsen. In the matter of one's general psychological functioning, people either grow healthier psychologically as they age, or they will deteriorate.

The most critical factor in the development and maintenance of mental health is the *quality of the individual's self-concept*—what the individual has learned to believe is true about himself as a person. A person's self-concept is formed in early childhood and is the primary element in determining the direction and quality of life. Sixty percent of all people live with a negative self-concept, at varying degrees of impairment, and most of them are unaware of it or just accept it as their only possible reality. Many others are aware but believe that feeling bad about one's self is "normal." It may be the norm, but it is not healthy. *A negative self-concept is at the base of, and a major part of, most mental illnesses.*

The Quality of Mental Health Treatment: A Wake-up Call

Historically, research into the effectiveness of psychological treatment, across a wide spectrum of theory and practice, has identified only two elements that are deemed critical to the success of any form of mental health treatment. These critical elements are the *level of mental health and the corresponding clinical skill set of the therapist, counselor, or helper.* Common sense tells the reader that these factors are critical for the successful treatment of mental illness.[1]

Unfortunately, across the broad field of mental health treatment, and at all levels of certification, there is little if any accountability for the mental health worker's level of mental health or clinical competency. Throughout its history the profession of psychology has minimized or ignored their importance to treatment outcome. It has always been assumed that if a person is intellectually educated, he or she is mentally sound and will be interpersonally competent. The reality is that mental health and interpersonal competence are not mutually inclusive with any level of formal education or training.

For people seeking mental health treatment, moving from being mentally ill to being mentally healthy requires obtaining help from someone who knows what mental health is—someone who is mentally healthy, and therefore has the knowledge and experience of *being* what the treatment goal is. Nevertheless, this idea of the helper being more mentally healthy than the person seeking treatment is not a principle or requirement in the field of mental health treatment or in its educational institutions. It is just assumed.

To become a more credible, effective, and respected discipline, the field of psychology must change its narrow focus on pathology, as well as its exclusion of any significant emphasis on mental health and preventive education. It must also hold itself more accountable for the quality of treatment rendered to the public. Above all, psychology must identify the characteristics, values, and abilities that define mental health. Psychology, to be effective, must be a leader

---

1 See Allen E. Bergin and Sol L. Garfield, , Sol L, *Handbook of Psychotherapy and Behavior Change* New York: John Wiley & Sons, 299-334.

in establishing the tenets of what it means to be a mentally sound, responsible, and competent human being and what it means to be mentally healthy, responsible, and competent at a societal level.

This book is an endeavor seeking to forward these goals by discussing the nature of mental health and its developmental essentials. Historical and current treatment philosophy and treatment methods are also critical issues that must be included in the discussion.

It is my position that, in the long run, the best treatment for mental illness is to prevent it, as much as possible, through psychological and interpersonal education. However, preventive psychological education is not a priority or even evident to any great degree. Therefore, the general public knows little about the psychological domain of their lives and still sees psychology as a mystery and mental illness as something that happens to other people.

Preventive education in areas such as developing a positive self-concept, effective parenting philosophy and related skills, relationship building, developing and nurturing emotional intimacy, and learning to accept and nurture psychological change, whether caused by crisis or other life events that are common to us all, are just a few of the areas where the elements and skills of mental health could be taught. A better-informed public would also go far in improving the quality of treatment because there would be greater accountability of the professional helper. As it is now, a psychologically naive and vulnerable patient most always blames himself for treatment failure.

Common sense tells us that *identifying mental illness* has to be predicated on *knowing what mental health is.* How can a counselor help someone achieve a goal like the state of mental health if he has not identified and specified its characteristics? Putting aside incompetence, in large part, the professional helper's treatment failures lie in their avoidance of what constitutes mental health. They are left to provide "treatment" with no direction or standards for success. Instead of having clear goals for reaching mental health, the treatment community relies on vague terms such as "improvement in the quality of life." Without specifying the characteristics of mental health, the labeling of any particular behavior as mentally unhealthy is nothing more than arbitrary and capricious.

This book is also a challenge to the profession of psychology, to be a leader in society and an agent of mental health both at a societal level and at the level of the individual. It is also an examination and critique of psychology's successes and failures in the treatment of mental illness. My hope is that it sparks a discussion among professionals as to the need for improvement in the quality of treatment rendered and the overall philosophy and goals of the helping profession. Most important is the critical need for psychology to define the elements of mental health. It's time to start prioritizing the prevention of mental illness through mental health education. To accomplish this task, a comprehensive and commonsense definition of mental health must be specified. Having a clear picture of the elements that comprise mental health would provide clarity and accountability for professional helpers and the people they treat.

1

The Current State of Mental Health Knowledge

Mental health is realized if an individual (or a society) develops into full psychological maturity according to the characteristics and laws of human nature. These natural laws are not part of a given social order but are basic, logical, and universally valid for all—irrespective of culture. How can we ever hope to ensure the mental health of our children if we cannot specify its elements, and be models of its essentials?

Defining Mental Health

The following are examples of how "mental health" is typically defined:

Oxford Dictionaries

noun

1. a person's condition with regard to their psychological and emotional well-being

Mental health is the foundation for emotions, thinking, communicating, learning, resilience and self-esteem. Mental health is also key to relationships, personal and emotional well-being and contributing to community or society. Many people who have a mental illness do not want to talk about it. But mental illness is nothing to be ashamed of!

Medlineplus.gov/mentalhealth.html

What is mental health? Mental health includes our emotional, psycho-logical, and social well-being. It affects how we think, feel, and act as we cope with life. It also helps determine how we handle stress, relate to others, and make choices. Mental health is important at every stage of life, from childhood and adolescence through adulthood.

Med Lexicon's Medical Dictionary

Emotional, behavioral, and social maturity or normality; the absence of a mental or behavioral disorder; a state of psychological well-being in which one has achieved a satisfactory integration of one's instinctual drives acceptable to both oneself and one's social milieu; an appropriate balance of love, work, and leisure pursuits.

Although the importance of mental health is noted in the above examples, these definitions leave the reader with no more knowledge about the elements of mental health than they had before reading them. The definitions make allusions not only to mental health's importance but also to the consequences of its absence. Overall, the reader is left not knowing what mental health really is or how he or she might compare to its mysterious elements. The definitions remind me of the politician whose rhetoric claims, "I value and stand for patriotism, family, and justice." His words tell us nothing about his true values. They are just words or categories of values that must be specified in order for the voter to agree or disagree.

In reality I have found that most people consider themselves to be mentally healthy even though they do not know what it is. It is only when they have been declared mentally impaired by some outside authority that they begin to care or wonder. On becoming involved with the treatment system, they are given a diagnosis as to the specific nature of their mental illness. Next, they are prescribed treatment and begin the mysterious process of therapy or counseling that will result in psychological change for the better. Individuals undergoing psychological treatment are told that regaining their mental health is accomplished by attacking the symptoms (behaviors) that explain the diagnosis they have been given. They are taught to view the relief of symptoms as the positive outcome of treatment. Therefore, *mental health is vaguely defined as the reduction of their symptoms.*

Psychological well-being is an unspoken value and goal we all have in common. However, do we know what it really is to be truly mentally healthy? No. Where is the written or spoken set of guidelines for identifying, developing, and maintaining mental health? How can an individual work effectively toward a goal that is defined as the absence of something? How can we ever hope to teach our children to be mentally healthy if we cannot specify even its most basic elements? Without this knowledge, being mentally healthy, teaching its content, and even treatment for mental illness are all left to chance and subjective interpretation because there is no clearly defined goal. And this is exactly what mankind does—leave mental health to chance. The field of psychology, the professional group with the responsibility for defining and teaching mental health, has traditionally abdicated from assuming this responsibility.

The most often discussed reason that the field of psychology has given for not establishing a unified position about the substance of mental health revolves around the field's early and continued focus on its obtaining credibility as a *hard science by adhering to the tenets of empiricism.*[1] In its efforts to increase its credibility, the field of psychology has traditionally declared itself to be a hard science like chemistry or biology, and therefore its focus must be on *objectivity and quantification.* In theory and practice, there is a concerted effort to eliminate the *subjective* and reject the notion that psychology is a soft science. This mistaken philosophical stance of assumed objectivity is unobtainable and impractical in psychology. Psychological research reflects its attempt to be objective. The research in large part contains artificial objectivity, which looks good on paper, if the reader does not look too closely, but the research quite often does not relate practically to the real world. In truth, the theoretical and applied practice of psychology is a subjective endeavor where there is no pure objec-

---

1   A system of acquiring knowledge that rejects all a priori knowledge and relies solely upon observation, experimentation, and induction.

tivity. To be effective, quality, not quantity, must always be central to the profession, at all levels, and especially at the treatment level.

As a result of their philosophical stance, the majority of psychological theorists and professional practitioners maintain the mistaken position that objectively defining mental health is impossible. The consensus is that defining mental health's content is too subjective and therefore too open to interpretation. Consequently, the generally accepted stance is that mental health exists when there is conformity to *cultural norms* within a society. This of course means, by default, that mental illness is a deviation from what your particular culture has defined as the accepted norms of thinking and behavior. I guess we are supposed to ignore the obvious irrationality, injustice, and even tyranny that can be perpetrated by either a dysfunctional minority in power or by the majority because of ignorance.

Today, the majority of psychology professionals continue to take the traditional and professionally safer position of avoiding the issue of defining and codifying the elements that describe mental health. In doing so, they maintain their illusion of objectivity. They also avoid offending the general public and anyone of authority who might be threatened. I agree that to take a stand on the nature of mental health that challenges current beliefs is a risky venture in any setting. As a matter of fact, it takes courage for an individual to stand up for what he believes to be true, especially when he is confronting majority opinion. However, one of the major characteristics of a mentally healthy individual or group is that courage is a primary motivator in their lives.

There is another reason behind psychology's failure to provide any constructive positive direction in establishing a unified or evolving position on the elements that constitute mental health. In addition to not offending the relevant authorities or the populace, the only other self-evident reason for not naming the elements of mental health is that they do not know or are unable to see the elements because of their own psychological deficits.

The failure to achieve, or even value, a unified position on the nature of mental health contributes to the growing chaos in our country. It also contributes to society's undervaluing mental health and treatment for mental illness. Ever-increasing mental illness, polarization, racism, entitlement, and collective irrationality are rapidly becoming our societal norms. America is a divided society where everyone can and does create their own truth. Individuals and groups choose facts that seem to support their beliefs and reject any opposing relevant facts.

As a society, we are struggling to accept people's right to believe differently, despite the biased or irrational nature of their beliefs. For example: The term "diversity" is a term that is evoked often in recent times. *We must be accepting of diversity, meaning people who are different from us. They have a right to be who they want to be and behave in ways they choose to. We need to respect them despite their difference.*

On the surface there seems to be nothing wrong with the idea of respecting diversity. We should all respect each other as *human beings of equal value and deserving of equal rights*. We should also respect others' rights to hold different opinions and beliefs. However, *this right is not unconditional*. We should not abandon reasoned truth as a standard. Diversity does not mean everyone can have their own facts and their own truth, especially when it comes to the nature of mental health. Accepting diversity does not mean that there is no right or wrong, no functional or dysfunctional, and therefore anything someone believes must be accepted as truth. Diversity also does not mean that there are multiple truths in regard to anything. It does not mean that just because someone has an opinion or a feeling that he is right. Real truth will always be the product of reasoned thinking.

In reality, diversity essentially means *respect for the person*, not agreement with anything he says or does. It means respect and equal rights and fair treatment for all people regardless of race, culture, or gender. Instead, the meaning of and use of the term "diversity" has been distorted to fit anyone's subjective idea of truth. This distortion of what is truth has permeated society to the point that few will stand up and disagree with irrational words or behavior in fear of being attacked by some faction that feels offended.

In the area of mental health, the profession of psychology needs to lead in establishing the tenets of mental health through reasoned thinking, then lead the movement to make it the norm. To accomplish this lofty task, psychology will have to stand up to society for what mental health is and identify its true causes, instead of being an agent of the status quo satisfied with profiting from treating individual pathology and ignoring the role of societal beliefs and practices as contributors to mental illness.

Formal Research about Mental Health

Inquiry into the elements that constitute mental health has not been completely disregarded. One notable and groundbreaking early effort to separate the concept of mental health from mental illness was Marie Jahoda's *Current Concepts of Positive Mental Health*, published in 1958 as the first in a series of monographs published by the Joint Commission on Mental Illness and Health. In her research, Jahoda presented a comprehensive review and discussion of elements considered to be present in those deemed mentally healthy. The author and her associates identified six major factors that contribute to a description of a mentally healthy individual:

1. (the valence of the) attitudes of the individual toward himself (self-concept, self-worth, self-efficacy);

2. (the) degree to which (an) individual realizes his potentialities through action (degree of self-development);

3. (the degree of) unification of function in the individual's personality, (the ability to integrate knowledge into a functional whole—as in the integration of thought and feeling);

4. (the) individual's degree of independence of social influences (autonomy);

5. how realistically the individual sees the world around him (reality orientation);

6. (the) ability to take life as it comes and master it (the ability one displays in meeting life's challenges and crises and transcending them);

Jahoda's research was a good beginning toward describing the characteristics of mental health. Her findings point to the importance of several factors that can be grouped into two major interdependent categories:

1. elements that have to do with beliefs and attitudes toward the self; and

2. cognitive and behavioral abilities.

Based on Jahoda's conclusions, a healthy self-concept includes one's degree of perceived self-worth and the actual degree of independence achieved from the attitudes and opinions of others. Unfortunately, Jahoda's work has been largely ignored.

During the twentieth century, there were other notable contributions to man's understanding of himself in relation to his mental health. The work of these researchers and practitioners has contributed invaluable insight as to the nature of mental health. Their insights, although acknowledged as contributions to the science of psychology, have been ignored, devalued, and worse—forgotten by the professional psychological community.

These notables include Bertrand Russell, Ayn Rand, Nathaniel Branden, Erich Fromm, Carl Rogers, and Robert R. Carkhuff. Others have made important contributions, but these stand out in my experience. These individuals, philosophers, and psychologists sought to isolate the substance of what it means to be mentally healthy. Their work provided ideas important to the generation of a comprehensive description of mental health for individuals and for societies. Why has their work been ignored or devalued? What factors keep professional psychological leaders from acting on this knowledge and developing standards of mental health, programs for the prevention of mental illness, and more basically, searching for and acknowledging the real causes of mental illness? It is my contention that the cause of the persistent failure to perceive, comprehend, value, and apply this knowledge is the level of mental health evident in those charged with doing the work.

Erich Fromm, in *The Sane Society*,[2] described the mentally healthy person as one who lives productively by the principles of love, reason, and *faith in his self*. He maintained that when all is as it should be, the normal development of a healthy individual proceeds according to the natural characteristics and laws of human nature. Through the gradual experience of an evolving self and responding change in the perception of the world, an individual develops objectivity and reason and builds a sense of independent identity and a functional knowledge of internal and external reality. Fromm's viewpoint is based on the assumption that, as in any other problem, there are right and wrong—satisfactory and unsatisfactory—solutions to the problem of human existence. Mental health is realized if man develops into full maturity accordingly.[3] These natural characteristics and laws are not part of a given social order but are basic, universal, and valid for all regardless of culture. Mental illness consists in the failure of such natural development to occur.

One of the most significant contributors to understanding the nature of mental health is Nathaniel Branden. His seminal work, *The Psychology of Self-Esteem*, centered on the nature and importance of self-esteem in establishing and maintaining mental health. He maintains that in order to deal with reality successfully—to pursue and achieve the values that life requires—a man needs self-esteem. He needs to feel confident of his self-efficacy and self-worth. He needs to feel and believe that he has value as a person equal to anyone.

Branden viewed mental illness as a *thinking disorder* where the root problem is always the mind's alienation from reality. The individual's alienation is both about the external reality of the objective world and his internal reality of his own self-perceptions. This individual lives in a world of cognitive and emotional separation from his self and objective reality. He resides in a personal world of irrational thinking, irrational emotions, and irrational actions. These are all symptoms of mental illness.

Branden made a very strong case with regard to man's cognitive responsibilities that contribute to his mental health. He begins

---

2   Erich Fromm, *The Sane Society*, (New York: Fawcett Publications, 1955).
3   Fromm, *The Sane Society*, p.270.

with asserting that existence alone sets a standard for man. His very survival requires *rationality (reasoned thinking), psychological independence, honesty, integrity, justice, productiveness, and pride.* Basic to developing these characteristics is the individual's connection to reality—the awareness, acceptance, and actually living of functional truth.

Rationality is the unreserved commitment to the accurate perception of reality, to the acceptance of reasoned thinking as an absolute—as one's only effective guide to constructive knowledge, values, and action.

To realize *psychological independence,* Branden maintained that the individual must take responsibility for his own existence and learn to rely on his own mind and judgment to identify truth.

Honesty is a refusal to seek values by faking reality, by evading the distinction between the real and the unreal.

Integrity is loyalty in action to the judgment of one's own consciousness.

Justice is the practice of identifying people for what they are and treating them accordingly—of rewarding or condemning their actions and traits of character.

Productiveness is the act of supporting one's existence by translating one's thought into reality, of setting one's goals and working for their achievement, of bringing knowledge or goods into existence.

Pride is the pleasure taken about one's self in response to achievements. It is also the dedication to achieving one's highest potential in one's character and in one's life. It is also the refusal to be a sacrificial fodder for the goals of others.[4]

Branden maintained that an individual whose cognitive contact with reality is unbreached will have perceptions, judgments, and evaluations of himself and the outside world that are free of distortions. He will be able and willing to look at any facts that are relevant to him and his welfare. He will display the cognitive characteristics of rationality, objectivity, and open-mindedness. He will be able to consciously consider all relevant facts but reserve the right to make

---

4   Nathaniel Branden, *The Psychology of Self-Esteem,* Nash Publishing, 1969., p.116.

final judgments about what is true. As this individual's thinking matures, it becomes more and more complex. Through a process of open-minded experience, formal learning, and continued psychological growth, the mentally healthy person's mind develops the ability to form abstract concepts and principles. Branden concluded that only reasoned thinking can judge what is or is not objectively in man's self-interest.

Branden's, Jahoda's, and Fromm's valuable contributions were all published more than fifty years ago. Sadly, they have been largely ignored, except by the occasional tenacious graduate student who discovers them.

In a more current research article, George E. Vaillant posed the question, *Positive Mental Health: Is There a Cross-Cultural Definition?*[5] In this article Vaillant surveyed research about mental health over the past half century. Based on this research, he suggested seven conceptually distinct models of positive mental health:

1. conceptualized as being above normal;

2. regarded as the presence of multiple human strengths;

3. conceptualized as maturity;

4. seen as the dominance of positive emotions;

5. conceptualized as high socioemotional intelligence;

6. viewed as subjective well-being; and

7. conceptualized as resilience.

After presenting historical research that supported each of these views, Vaillant concluded that they all had merit and that a definition of mental health must therefore be multifaceted. He did state emphatically that, "We can enhance mental health only through cognitive, behavioral and psychodynamic education." At best, this study provided some specific areas for further investigation. However,

---

5 George E. Vaillant, "Positive Mental Health: Is There a Cross-Cultural Definition?" *World Psychiatry* 11, no. 2 (June 2012), https://doi.org/10.1016/j.wpsyc.2012.05.006.

Vaillant's conclusion was that defining mental health clearly is a difficult undertaking.

In another study about the nature of mental health, Laurie A. Manwell and associates made an attempt to find consensus as to a definition of mental health. The question posed in the article asked, what are the core concepts of mental health? A survey questionnaire was sent to fifty people with expertise in the field of mental health from eight different countries. The results of the survey were validated at a consensus meeting of fifty-eight clinicians, researchers, and people with "lived experience."

Their primary conclusion was that the core concepts of mental health are "highly dependent on the *empirical* frame used," and that it would be necessary to understand these empirical frames in order to develop a useful consensus definition for diverse populations. This is another way to say that mental health is different in different cultures. Participants in the survey were able to generate a few core characteristics related to individual mental health that are worth mentioning:

- the capacity and ability for choice in interacting with society;

- the capacity to effectively deal with and/or create change in oneself;

- having a positive subjective experience of self;

- the ability to choose one's level of social participation;

- having the ability to disconnect by choice, as opposed to being excluded (e.g., having the capacity and ability to reject social, legal, and theological practices); and

- having an above average ability for individual autonomy and control over the self.[6]

This study was a bit more insightful about mental health than most research in that its conclusions focused on positive attributes

6   Laurie A. Manwell et al., "What Is Mental Health? Evidence Towards a New Definition from a Mixed Methods Multidisciplinary International Survey," *BMJ Open* 5, no. 6 (2015).

identifiable as mentally healthy in an individual. The research sites several characteristics that are reflective of mental health. First, and probably the most important, is the need to have a *positive subjective experience of self*. Second is the ability to be autonomous in the sense of having control over oneself and having your own mind as the source for judgments instead of being controlled by external authority. Third, the study points to the importance of being able to *experience and create psychological change* in a successful fashion.

However, the research falls short because it does not attempt to explain the origin of these characteristics, how they are created. Where does one get a positive self-concept? What allows a person to be autonomous, to believe he has the right to make his own judgments? What makes a person able to handle change better than the next person, or to know how to create and manage change within himself? I think overall the study points the discussion about mental health in a good direction, at least in a partial way.

I do not agree with the study's conclusion that the core concepts of mental health are "highly dependent on the empirical frame used." I am assuming that what they mean by an empirical frame of reference was that mental health is culture dependent. If so, I disagree. To my way of thinking, elements or characteristics that describe mental health should and could be readily understood by anyone in any culture. For example, the idea of self-concept, how much a person truthfully values himself as a person, translates universally. The factors that enabled the creation, development, and conservation of a positive self-concept are also clear and therefore should be understandable to any frame of reference.

Overall, the work of these researchers provided a beginning in the form of a few valuable insights concerning the nature of mental health. However, their work has been largely overlooked. Instead, the field of psychology has continued to emphasize and focus on pathology. If psychology wants to remain relevant as a human science, it must seriously consider changing its focus from primarily a pathological perspective to a broader and more reality-based concentration that includes focusing on the nature of mental health.

The profession of psychology also has a major responsibility to address the societal impediments to the development of mental health and one's ability to maintain mental health throughout one's lifetime. This responsibility would mean that the profession changes its present focus on treatment to a perspective that includes the necessity for prevention through education. Psychological education, to be effective, must include the elements of mental health and interpersonal competence.

Major Conclusions of Chapter One

How can we ever hope to teach our children to be mentally healthy if we cannot specify its elements?

To the majority of mental health professionals, defining mental health is considered a subjective process and its content is an open and flexible entity.

To date, the helping professions have failed to provide any constructive positive direction in establishing a unified or ununified position on the elements that constitute mental health.

The field of psychology, as the recognized authority on mental illness, has a leader's responsibility to identify and teach the elements and competencies that comprise mental health.

The profession of psychology also has a responsibility to address and effect change at the community and societal levels. The profession's relevance as a respected human science will depend on the field's assuming these broader responsibilities.

2

Psychology: Deficits in Philosophy and Methodology

There is a reason no one in the profession of psychology will use the word "cure." The speaker would have to know and state what cured is—what mental health is. Psychology as a profession needs to stop supporting the pathological status quo and start speaking out for what is right and mentally healthy for us all.

Deficits in Philosophy and Treatment

While it is true that much has been accomplished in the science of psychology since its inception in the nineteenth century, there is much it has not accomplished. Psychology's deficits in focus, methods, and competence are readily apparent in the increasing incidence and pervasiveness of mental illness in societies today.

Psychological theorists, professional academics, and practitioners in the field of mental health have historically limited their role to the identification and treatment of mental pathology. The vast majority of professional psychology practitioners have chosen to focus on identifying *behaviors as pathologies* and developing treatments for these behavioral *symptoms*. The behavior is seen as the root problem and therefore the target of treatment. Deeper psychological issues that may exist are ignored or not adequately addressed. In my estimation, the industry has allowed this self-limiting and largely ineffective philosophy to prevail. The major consequence of this philosophical position has been to slow the growth of psychology as a viable and trusted profession.

One current example of mistaken thinking by professionals who have arbitrarily identified a behavior as a mental illness is "road rage." Road rage, or *intermittent explosive disorder*, has been identified as a mental illness. Intermittent explosive disorder involves repeated sudden episodes of impulsive, aggressive, violent behavior or angry verbal outbursts in which an individual's reaction is grossly out of proportion to the situation. The descriptive behaviors of this illness include: temper tantrums, verbal tirades, heated arguments, shouting, slapping, shoving or pushing, physical fights, property damage, and threatening or assaulting people or animals. All of these can occur in the context of operating a motor vehicle or in the context of any relationship. The prescribed treatment for this illness is "talk therapy and medication." Actually, not being able to control aggressive or violent behavior is a *symptom of a much more significant underlying problem*, usually having to do with being emotionally immature and self-centered to a negative extreme. *At an even deeper level lies a lifelong negative self-concept.*

So, what is the definition of mental health? The accepted definition of mental health remains as simply the *absence of identified pathology.* That is obviously a definition of what it is not instead of what it is. *The most egregious omission of the profession is the failure to identify the characteristics or elements that constitute mental health.*

The historical emphasis on identifying and treating only the behavioral symptoms of mental illness has resulted in too many erroneous, ineffective, and contradictory treatment theories and practices. Within the helping professions, there is no real accountability for treatment validity, therapist competence, or any unified standards for successful treatment. Pervasive incompetence is the norm for mental health practitioners.

Behind closed doors a therapist, counselor, or helper in any position or level of practice can *do anything they want and call it treatment.* Validity, quality, and outcome of treatment are not assessed. Clinical skills are assumed based on the educational degree held by the practitioner or, in too many cases, conformity to the program of organizational authorities. Treatment methods are assumed to be valid because some higher authority has decreed their use. Success or failure is not addressed. Helpers may or may not have had any significant amount of clinical training.

Another major factor underlying treatment failure, clinician incompetence, and absence of accountability for treatment outcome is the fact that *the incidence of mental health among mental health practitioners, at any level of education or amount of experience, is not any greater than the general public they are treating.* Acquiring an academic degree or being certified at any level does not make a person clinically competent. A clinician's competence comes from his level of mental health and the resulting quality of his interpersonal competence.[1] Like everyone else, helpers, professional or lay, identify problems and attempt to solve them, at the level they themselves understand them. A therapist cannot lead anyone to a level of psychological functioning that he has not achieved for himself. In the psychological domain, a person cannot teach that which he is not.

Therapy, counseling, or helping in the most basic sense is about guiding an individual to some experienced state of being that they have been unable to understand and achieve on their own. If the helper has not achieved this level of understanding and experienced achieving similar goals, he cannot lead someone to a state of being unknown to himself. Stated more concretely, a professional helper cannot help someone become more psychologically healthy than he himself is.

Quantity vs. Quality in Mental Health Treatment

The current philosophy about treating veterans provides an example of ineffective treatment philosophy and methods. Federal treatment policy places emphasis on the *quantity of contacts* with veterans instead of the *quality of treatment* rendered. However, because of high demand for treatment, actual contact time is strictly

---

1   Allen E. Bergin and Sol L. Garfield, eds., *Handbook of Psychotherapy and Behavior Change* (New York: John Wiley & Sons, 1971, 1978).

regulated to "treat as many as possible" in the time available. Treatment for veterans within the Veterans Administration (VA) programs is effectively reduced to token short clinical visits and prescribing psychotropic drugs to possibly relieve symptoms. The large numbers of contacts are touted as evidence of quality treatment.

This practice is partly a reaction to being overwhelmed by the large number of veterans who need help, and the paucity of money and staff needed to render adequate treatment. While it's true that the VA's programs are overwhelmed with people needing mental health services, it does no one any good to equate the numbers of people seen with successful treatment. Well-intentioned mental health practitioners are hamstrung by time-consuming and useless bureaucratic policies and regulations.

The underlying and disregarded cause of the Veterans Administration's less-than-adequate health delivery system is that mental health and mental illness treatment are of low priority in our society as a whole and therefore a low priority for our government. The problems ascribed to the VA's programs are exacerbated by the fact that many—if not most—of mentally afflicted veterans had existing mental health issues before they enlisted and were ignored. It is easier to blame the experience of war and diagnose post-traumatic stress disorder. That way we can continue to avoid taking responsibility and action to stem the pervasive presence of mental illness in society.

Not taking responsibility for the quality of our mental health is a cultural problem. Instead of a genuine responsible interest and focus on mental health, our culture's actual lived values focus upon the acquisition of material goods and attempting to look as physically young as possible and to look good physically to others. These superficial goals dominate culture. Our concern for ourselves is limited to the satisfaction of our immediate "needs." We claim values and virtues that we do not live and live values and resulting behaviors that we do not claim.

Those who have more money are concerned about their investment portfolio, and others not as financially blessed contribute to the profits of finance companies by living on next month's money instead of last month's earnings. Principles, values, ethics, and morality are given token attention but have little to do with our real daily lives. Knowledge and concern about the quality of our mental health is given token attention. The rising tide of mental illness that affects all our lives remains under the radar, too, as part of the vast unknowable and uncontrollable. Our collective and individual knowledge and concern about our mental health is left in the hands of external authorities and experts.

Mistaken Beliefs about the Causes and Treatment of Addiction

Addiction is a disease—people catch it from open bottles.

Let's examine another illustration of mistaken philosophy and treatment methods: addiction. The usual treatment process for those cursed with an addictive "disease" includes being dried out in an expensive treatment center, if the person can afford it, then shuttled off to the appropriate Alcoholics Anonymous (AA) organization for further "treatment." To be viewed as responsible, the person is required to submit to the AA a belief structure and program. The new member is required to accept that he has a lifelong "disease," and that there is nothing he can do to be cured. If the individual does not conform, he is deemed in denial of his disease and doomed to self-destruction.[2]

The misconception of seeing the behavior as the problem to treat is evident in the treatment of addiction. I will use addiction to alcohol as my example, but it is the same for any addictive behavior. The behavior of excessive or irresponsible drinking is mistakenly labeled a "mental disease," and the focus is on controlling or changing the *behavior*. Experience should have taught the professional community the error of their thinking, but it has not. The consequences of this faulty assumption and treatment philosophy are evidenced in the

---

2   See a complete discussion of addiction treatment, an objective viewpoint, by reading Stanton Peele's volume, *The Diseasing of America: Addiction Treatment Out of Control*, 1989. See also my article, *Addiction as a Social Construction: A Postempirical View, Journal of Psychology* 127, no. 5 (June 1993).

well-known statistics that report that only 7 percent of those receiving treatment are being successfully helped.[3] One might ask, what percentage of people that do not receive treatment decide to be psychologically responsible and stop drinking on their own? I suspect it's more than seven percent.

Contemporary confusing and contradictory beliefs about addiction, which are inherent in AA's 12-step model, are examples of the human propensity to retain and reinforce faulty beliefs. For example, the 12-step model supports the beliefs that the disease is not caused by the individual, it is uncontrollable and incurable. Belief structures concerning the individual's responsibility for causing, controlling, and curing addiction to alcohol include a *community consensus* of opinion, which, on the surface, promotes externalization of responsibility as part of its structure. However, despite externalization of the responsibility, the addict is placed in a double bind by being held responsible for abstaining from an uncontrollable and incurable condition that is caused by an unknown force.

If successful in staying in recovery, the addict must admit powerlessness over the disease, live in fear of its return, and remain dependent through perpetual membership in a support group. He must also give credit for any success to the model and the group. However, if treatment fails, the individual is both responsible for the resumption of drinking and yet is not responsible because alcoholism is an uncontrollable and incurable disease. The 12-step model fails to provide any hope or avenue for normalcy through the incorporation of self-responsibility and independence from a support group.

This kind of irrational thinking coupled with contradicting research and facts about addiction have perpetuated the conclusion that irresponsible drinking is a disease that cannot be cured. The only "treatment" seen as viable is to place addicts in perpetual groups that will help them stay in recovery and "survive one day at a time." Once referred to these groups, which are created and run by nonprofessionals who are "victims" of the same "disease," the individual is

---

3 Stanton Peele, *The Diseasing of America: Addiction Treatment Out of Control*, 78.

left on his own to deal with a quasi-religious contradictory program that places him in a psychological double bind.

In the 12-step addiction treatment program, it is preferred if not required that the sponsor, counselor, or helper should have the mental illness or "disease" they are treating. Only addicts are deemed able to help addicts. Unfortunately, most helping professionals agree with this belief, but only after the professional treatment community has exhausted the diseased victim's insurance benefits.

A *nonaddict* counselor is perceived as lacking an empathic understanding of the addict's experience. Such contentions are patently false and therefore destructive to many who could benefit from real clinical treatment for their addiction instead of perpetual dependency and acceptance of a lifetime of "one day at a time" survival as all that can be expected. People with addictions who want to take personal responsibility for themselves seek help to identify the real underlying psychological problems and want to rise above dependence on a program claiming that survival is all they can expect in their future. In most cases, this will be a nonaddict professional that is competent enough to focus on the real underlying pathology and is also willing to challenge the validity of tenets held by AA programs. Unfortunately, this level of skilled professional is a rarity.

Truth be told, AA's treatment philosophy mimics that of traditional religions. The addict must accept their belief structure or be "damned to hell in a handbasket." Countless individuals, addicts, and nonaddicts are forced into 12-step programs by all types of legal authorities who deem them necessary or perhaps a punishment. Once referred, the new member better at least pretend to believe in the program or else face worse social and legal consequences.

The underlying truth about excessive drinking and about any other addictive behavior is that the addict perceives their behavior, such as drinking, as a viable solution to their perceived problems. They are typically unaware of their deeper psychological issues. In reality, addictive behaviors are attempts designed to help the individual *escape from themselves*. Why would it be necessary to escape from themselves? The answer is always because they do not like who they are. *Again, this is a self-concept issue.*

Effective treatment for addictive disorders must go way beyond a superficial treatment methodology that focuses on the individual's behavior as the disease or disorder, which they are powerless to change and therefore must rely on day-to-day survival and dependence on others similarly afflicted, acting as an externalized self-support object. Instead, effective treatment must be aimed at the true cause of the addictive disorder. The fundamental cause of addictive disorders is a psychological disorder of the self. Self-disorders are thinking disorders. Any relevant therapy to addiction must address the individual's core beliefs about himself as a person. It is these core beliefs that determine every thought, every feeling, and every action taken or not taken by the individual. For treatment to be viable, it must address these negative core beliefs. The individual's irrational and destructive core beliefs must be made conscious in order to effect changing them. Changing these core beliefs to more rational, realistic, and beneficial beliefs is essential to the change process.[4]

Psychotropic Drugs as Treatment

Another illustration of ineffective and potentially dangerous treatment philosophy is the growing preference and reliance on psychotropic drugs as the preferred form of treatment. Psychology is more and more following the practice of prescribing drugs. In the general practice of physical medicine, there is plenty of evidence in American society of the inappropriate and dangerous practice of prescribing drugs indiscriminately. The opioid crisis has helped to produce a national epidemic of addiction that has reached drastic proportions. Many thousands of people die from addiction overdose each year because they are told by the professional medical community that opioids are not harmful.

Within the mental health treatment community, with the advent of psychotropic drugs, actual interpersonal therapy is increasingly viewed as an unnecessary supportive option to drug therapy. Instead, finding the right drug or drugs to allay a multitude of symptoms

---

4 C. Franklin Truan, *My Enemy—Myself: Overcoming Your Self-Defeating Mind* (Tucson AZ: Wheatmark, 2014).

is the goal of treatment. This has always been the approach of psychiatrists, but now psychologists, who traditionally have practiced verbal interpersonal therapy, the "talking cure," are attempting to obtain the credentials to prescribe medications. As of now, only psychiatrists and other licensed physicians can prescribe medications.

In actuality, psychotropic medications *treat only symptoms,* and they are effective only 30 percent of the time in accomplishing the reduction of any symptoms. Treatment of this type is a trial-and-error guessing game. Try a drug that has worked for some people with the same diagnosis. If it doesn't work, try another one. If that one works even a little to relieve symptoms but has some undesirable side effects, prescribe another drug to alleviate the side effect. So forth and so on. Interpersonal treatment (therapy) is usually minimal or absent. Sure, lip service is given to seeking therapy or counseling while receiving medications, but in practice that's all it is. Psychotropic drugs are widely prescribed by all types of medical practitioners without regard for an accurate diagnosis, knowledge of the drug's efficacy, or referral to a therapist.

The bottom line is that in the mental health arena, symptoms (behaviors) are not the illness. They are just signs of an underlying mental problem. Even if drugs can reduce symptoms, they do not address the cause of the symptoms. Real psychological treatment that leads to real psychological change requires verbal therapy and education conducted by a reasonably healthy and competent individual. Through adequate interpersonal exploration, the real problem can be identified and the appropriate intervention strategies employed. The use of psychotropic drugs should only be used when absolutely necessary and only on a temporary basis. An overuse of psychotropic medication impedes the therapeutic process both physically and psychologically. Drugs should never be the primary treatment modality.

A Rational Subjective Code of Ethics and Morality

Psychology, as a subjective science, must take a stand on the nature and elements of mental health at least to the degree that it has subjectively decided to focus on and prioritize what mental illness is. The continued avoidance as to the specific nature of mental health is an irresponsible and indefensible position. What is healthy or unhealthy, right or wrong, or constructive or disruptive to the nature and needs of human beings should not be left in the hands of those traditional authorities with subjective self-interests, enabled by the continuation of traditions that nurture ignorance, division, and destruction. Psychology's goals must center on the psychological advancement of the individual man and mankind as a whole. To do so, it must focus on and take a stand on morality and ethics that contribute to the mental health of individuals and are universal in that they apply to all.

> Morality is a code of values accepted by choice. Moral values are chosen values of a fundamental nature in that they shape man's character and life course.

> —Leonard Peikoff, *Objectivism:*
> *The Philosophy of Ayn Rand*[5]

It is obvious to me that man needs an objective code of ethical/ moral values. The code would define and support the development and maintenance of mental health. However, theorists and practitioners in the field of psychology have consistently maintained that science and ethics and morality are mutually exclusive. They maintain that morality and/or ethics are the province of faith and not the business of psychology. Further, they view morality and ethics as subjective and the exclusive right of the individual. It is accepted practice that the therapist should treat his patients without challenging their subjective moral beliefs, even if they are irrational or destructive.

I believe the definition of morality and ethics, and the distinction between the two, is necessary for the reader's understanding:

Morality: what is perceived to be right and wrong, initially emanates from external culture, usually from sources considered

---

5 Leonard Peikoff, *Objectivism: The Philosophy of Ayn Rand,* (New York: Penguin Books, 1993) 214.

authorities, particularly parents. Because these beliefs are learned during the formation of the primitive-self, they are adopted and incorporated as truth in a child's mind. If they are to be retained into adulthood, they must be evaluated through reasoning for validity. Moral beliefs learned in early life are the most firmly implanted beliefs. They are therefore the most difficult beliefs to change, even if they are irrational, psychologically limiting, and harmful to the individual and others.

Ethical morality: Individual ethical morality takes the form of meta-self principles created and adopted independently within an individual as he advances toward adulthood. This process will be a continual process throughout his lifespan as experience and psychological maturation occurs. Ethical principles of a mentally healthy person are the result of objective reasoned thinking. They do not emanate from emotions and are not controlled by them. A mentally healthy individual is consciously aware of his ethical principles and is self-accountable for actually living according to them.

Ethical behavior, another source of what is right and wrong, may also originate from outside sources. As an example, the ethical principles for psychologists seek to define what is proper behavior in the practice of psychology.

A person who needs therapy and seeks it is a person who is experiencing psychological pain and confusion. His beliefs, including professed and actual morality, are the source of his distress. His mind is a collection of both rational and irrational beliefs, but he cannot distinguish truth. His divided mind is at odds with itself. His beliefs are foggy, weak, and contradictory. The individual's experience of his own mind is that of distrust of its processes and content, and therefore he exists with a lack of faith in his mind to know truth. He has lost faith in himself.

To be effective, the therapist must address the issue of confused and faulty thinking in the patient. (We are of course assuming that the therapist is of sound mind, rational, and lives a functional code of ethical morality.) In the therapeutic process, irrational beliefs, flexible values, contradictions between thought and action, and harmful behavior must all be addressed. To ignore the beliefs of the patient is to ignore reality. The individual's beliefs take the form of principles, values, ethics, and beliefs about morality. They all must be open to critical clinical evaluation. The content and quality of an individual's beliefs are at the very heart of mental illness and mental health.

To be clinically effective, therapists and counselors must address the patient's beliefs, all of which are based on subjective thinking, that are potentially biased and entwined with morality. Therefore, it is my contention that psychology, a soft science, must incorporate addressing the functionality of all belief structures of the patient. Excluding anything that is considered ethics or morality from the treatment process is a denial of reality and a recipe for therapeutic failure.

In reality, neutrality or objectivity in the therapeutic process is not possible for the therapist either. Therapists have their own set of beliefs that are always present and affect the course and quality of treatment. Therefore, to be effective, the therapist must possess and practice a mentally sound code of ethics and morality. This is a necessity if he is to provide additive direction in the therapeutic process toward mental health. The therapist must know what a sound ethical code is, and that he possesses it, to be effective in helping others. It is a central feature of a mentally healthy individual. Common sense tells us that a therapist cannot lead someone to a place that he does not understand because he has not been there.

Finally, ethics and morality that are professed but not actually lived do not really exist. A mentally healthy individual will have a conscious set of principles, including those of an ethical and moral nature, and actually live them. This is true for all persons participating in a therapeutic endeavor.

In Summary

The incidence of mental health is no more prevalent in the portion of the population that treats mental illness than it is in the rest of the general population.

As stated previously, to the professional field of psychology, *mental health is principally defined by both default and practice as the absence of recognized pathology.* Psychology theorists and practitioners have overwhelmingly chosen to focus not on the elements of mental health but rather on identifying mental pathologies and devising, for better or worse, treatments purporting to alleviate their symptoms.

Conspicuously absent in psychological literature is any widespread interest in the identification of elements that constitute mental health. In fact, the accepted stance is that it is not feasible to attempt to define it. Absent also is the construction of a comprehensive preventive philosophy about mental illness. In psychological research, training, and practice, professional concentration is primarily focused on mental processes and behaviors considered pathological by current societal beliefs.

The historical focus solely on aberrant behavior and pathologically based thinking served the profession well as a beginning point in the nineteenth and twentieth centuries for understanding human thought and behavior. However, the resulting creation and development of a plethora of theories and treatment modalities based on pathology has served only to broaden and entrench the field's outdated and mistaken focus. It is way past time for the field as a whole to reevaluate its overall philosophy and goals. Research into the effectiveness of all psychological theories and methods of psychological treatment has repeatedly concluded that just as many people get well waiting in line for treatment as those who *actually receive* it. The factors that make a qualitative difference in treatment outcome have consistently been identified to be the level of mental health and degree of interpersonal competency of the therapist or counselor.[6]

Specific needed goals for the profession of psychology include:

- identifying the elements that make an individual mentally healthy, including character traits, attitude about self and toward others, age-appropriate psychological character traits, and abilities and behaviors, just to name a few;

- assuring the mental health and competency of its profes-

---

6   Robert R. Carkhuff and Bernard G. Berenson, *Beyond Counseling and Therapy* (New York: Holt, Rinehart, and Winston, 1967), 227.

sional practitioners as well as the wide variety of nonprofessional helpers;

- identifying and teaching mental health competencies to groups who have a profound effect on the developing mental health of children (e.g., parents, teachers, lay counselors); and

- teaching mental health elements and competencies to the public using mass media as a means for reaching vast numbers of people.

The science of psychology has become a collection of diverse theories and methods that are characterized by their lack of demonstrated effectiveness. Psychology is, in actuality, a soft, subjective science still employing the hard science tenets of empiricism, and in doing so is increasingly threatening its consideration as a viable or effective science. It's well past time that the profession changes its philosophical position by moving to incorporate a more accurate and effective perception of itself. Subjectivity is already endemic to psychology at all levels, from theory to treatment. Why not own it consciously and work to be better at knowing when it introduces bias in our perceptions and behavior?

This change in philosophical approach must include the incorporation of being and perfecting the soft science that it is, while rationally holding itself accountable for being as objective as humanly possible. *To accomplish this, the skills of reasoning must be the primary cognitive method for establishing the best subjective truth in theorizing, methodology, and evaluation of effectiveness at the level of application.*

3

An Overview of Mental Health Characteristics at Different Stages of Life

This chapter presents an initial overview of what it means to be mentally healthy. A more comprehensive description of mental health and competency is presented in subsequent chapters. Presented first are some major characteristics of being mentally healthy, followed by examples of observed mental well-being and competence at several different developmental stages of life.

Characteristics of Mental Health

Four major characteristics of mentally healthy people:

- thinking and feeling good about who he is as a person—and being accurate;

- having a conscious and consistent connection to reality;

- trusting his mind's rational cognitive processes to provide him with truth; and

- being competent interpersonally, having the ability to get needs met—physical, intellectual, and psychological—and the ability to respond adequately to the needs of others.

More specific characteristics and competencies of mentally healthy individuals:

- consciously values and lives in functional reality, including objective reality and functional subjective reality as appropriate;

- thinks rationally and objectively, which enables effective self-evaluation of feelings, thinking content and processes, and beliefs;

- demonstrates reasoning and logic as the default thinking system, is conceptually open-minde—incorporating all relevant facts, not just those that are in agreement;

- trusts the processes of his own mind to sustain an accurate and objective connection to reality and displays a consistent ability to discern truth (self-efficacy);

- consciously formulates and lives rational beneficial principles that guide thinking and actions in all areas of life;

- consistently lives congruent and beneficial values;

- pursues physical, intellectual, and psychological self-development as a lifestyle, views living as a lifelong process of learning and becoming;

- physically, intellectually, and psychologically responsible (externally and internally);

- able to delay self-gratification;

- values and pursues achieving challenging goals to maintain meaning and purpose in life (e.g., the realization of psychological individuation and maturity);

- demonstrates a positive functional empathic connection with self and others;

- is tolerant of ambiguity and difference;

- has the ability to nurture and be nurtured—to love and be loved; and

- develops and maintains fulfilling and lasting quality relationships (e.g., establishes and maintains healthful relationships, including intimate ones), prevents problems and solves them effectively when they occur.

Mental Health in Different Stages of Life

Necessary Assumptions:

Developing and maintaining mental health is a lifelong process. An individual does not just achieve it, for instance, like earning a college degree and then pursuing other goals. Being mentally healthy changes throughout one's lifetime because we are always in a process of adaptation and forced change as we move through life and the many challenges it presents.

Mental health and mental illness are mostly learned. The majority of people are born with the capacity to be mentally sound; however, the primary determining factor in maintaining a healthful direction is the quality of their social environment. The quality of parenting or primary caregiving, and, to a lesser extent, the genetic makeup we inherit by chance, determine psychological health or illness. Additionally, psychological research has concluded that the most important factor in growing up to be a mentally healthy adult is the long-term continuous exposure and guidance received from at least one mentally healthy caregiver during childhood.

For the purpose of describing mental health at various stages of life, it is necessary to make the assumption that the primary caregivers have achieved a reasonable degree of mental health before conceiving a child. Primary caregivers who are mentally sound are able to model mental health. Modeling what it is to be mentally sound responds to a young child's primary mode of learning. However, this description of a mentally healthy setting is an ideal, the exception to the rule instead of the norm. I don't believe that anyone has had the experience of being reared by perfect parents. As humans we all have our flaws, and healthful parenting is itself a process of learning how to rear children. Only grandparents consider themselves expert.

Although it's unrealistic to *require* that parents must be mentally sound and interpersonally competent themselves to have and raise children, we can talk about and even advocate characteristics and interpersonal abilities that make people more capable of providing the psychological environment and interpersonal competencies that are necessary for healthful mental development.

First, for purposes of general description, parents can be divided into two groups: functional or dysfunctional. The first group is sufficiently mentally healthy, and are able to model mental health and respond appropriately to the psychological needs of a child at each developmental stage.

The other group of parents are themselves psychologically impaired to some degree, and therefore they are major contributors to psychological dysfunctionality in their offspring. There are many types of mental dysfunction that negatively influence normal psychological development in children. Because this book is not about mental illness, I will provide only one illustrative example of dysfunctional parenting because of mental impairment.

In keeping with one of the major themes in this book, my example will be about parents with negative self-concepts and their effect on the psychological development of their children. The foremost observation of an individual with a negative self-concept is that they are extremely self-focused. In plain terms this means that they are overinvolved in a negative manner with their own psychological problems. One type of dysfunctional parent will use the child in ways that respond to the parent's pathological needs. The child will be taught that his needs are not important and even that he as a person is not important unless he responds continuously to the needs of the psychologically impaired parent. The child becomes a servant to the parent's needs and becomes symbiotically attached to the parent and works constantly for the parent's approval, which the child misinterprets as love. Because of the symbiotic attachment to the parent, the child does not develop an independent identity. The child becomes pathologically dependent on the parent.

Another form of being excessively self-centered to the detriment of the child is to be physically or emotionally absent. For example, a mother or father consumed with achieving in a career has a perception of parenting as a necessary responsibility but with much less priority. Still another parent could be present most of the time but be so psychologically preoccupied with himself that he is unaware of the child's psychological needs. This is an example of a person who has no understanding of the ongoing developmental psychological needs of the child. The parent lacks the ability to empathically connect with the child. The child may be given everything else they need, such as food, a good education, and as much freedom as they want.

A child that does not receive empathy or genuine caring in the form of unconditional love, empathic understanding, quality time spent together, and appropriate limits on behavior will feel bad about themselves. In the most severe cases, a child will experience abandonment and blame himself. He is too young to understand that his bad thoughts and feelings about himself are because of what the parent or parents have failed to provide. To survive psychologically the child must repress these negative beliefs and feelings about himself.

To put it in brief form, parents and other primary care givers *teach their children who they are and what they do, for better or worse.* The old parental adage, "Don't do as I do, do as I say," never works. Children watch and learn what primary caregivers do and incorporate it as the way they should be. By the way, they also very quickly learn to use parental feelings and deficits against them in order to get what they want in the moment, regardless of how harmful it may be to their psychological development in the long run.

A normal child is self-focused and lives in the present. Accordingly, he is focused on his immediate needs, be they food, attention, or relief from physical or emotional discomfort. When a young child listens to his parents he hears only two things. He hears only the parent's feelings and what they actually do behaviorally in response to his behavior or even just his presence. Dysfunctional parents are typically unaware of their child's perceptions of their behavior.

The Developmental Facets of the Human Mind

Defining what mental health is, in a brief and concise manner, is challenging. It is problematic because it, like mental illness, is a multifaceted concept. In this chapter I am going to provide the reader with an initial glimpse into what mental health is. The characteristics and competencies that define mental health will be explored further throughout this book.

The content of characteristics representing mental health for a child will not be the same as that of a chronological adult. Acquiring and maintaining mental health is an ever-changing lifelong process, and therefore describing it must be accomplished by providing age-specific descriptions. Therefore, I will describe mental health characteristics and behaviors for five different age groups: an infant or very young child, a child of seven or eight years, a preteen or early teen of twelve or thirteen, an aspiring adult at age seventeen or eighteen, and, a psychologically maturing adult in their mid-30s.

To facilitate the reader's understanding of my descriptions of mental health at various ages, brief definitions of my terms for the psychological facets of the self in one's mind must be provided. They will be discussed in greater detail in succeeding chapters. The human mind can be divided into three interrelated developmental psychological entities. These entities are composed of subjective content, such as facts and beliefs; learned cognitive processes; and emotional processes and tendencies. The *primitive-self* is the first facet of the psychological self to develop, followed closely by the *surface-self*, then a slowly developing *meta-self* gradually emerges. At any given stage of development, these mental structures are interrelated and comprise the individual's perception of reality, his beliefs and feelings about himself, and his attitude toward life.

The *primitive-self* is the portion of the mind that is formed earliest in life. It is shaped during the first six years of life.

The *surface-self* is the portion of the mind that acts as the mind's agent that is presented to and interacts with the outside world.

The *meta-self* is the rational, objective, confident, competent, responsible, and eventually mature facet of the mind.

Mental Health: Age Two to Six, Infancy and Early Childhood

Fostering mental health in a newborn and a young child's primitive-self begins with the establishment of a positive self-concept— feeling good about one's self as a person. As described above, the quality of parenting provided is the major contributor to quality of a forming primitive-self. A positive self-concept, established in the first few years of life, provides the necessary psychological foundation for the continued cognitive and emotional development of an individual's mental health.

A primary caregiver who models mental health and has acquired the interpersonal knowledge and skills to respond in an age-appropriate psychological manner is instrumental in fostering a positive self-concept within the mind of a young child. Clinically this ability to respond helpfully and healthfully is referred to as *stage appropriate empathic responding*. The caregiver's ability to respond adequately and age appropriately is based on the level of their own mental health and their learned conceptual knowledge and applied skill in empathically responding to the needs and experience of others.

Being born to a parent or parents who are sufficiently mentally healthy and skilled at appropriate responding is in reality a chance occurrence. It is the province of a lucky few of us. Having the ability to respond in a psychologically appropriate manner to children has never been a requirement for having a child, and neither has the level of an aspiring parent's mental health. Nevertheless, the level of mental health and interpersonal competence of parents are the most critical factors in determining the child's successful acquisition of a positive secure sense of self. I will discuss, at a later point, additional knowledge and interpersonal competencies critical to effective parenting. It is important to note that the number of primary caregivers, or the amount of time spent with the child, is not the most critical factor in rearing a mentally healthy child. It is rather the mental health and quality of the interpersonal interactions between the primary caregivers and the child that matter most.

What are the characteristics of this child who was lucky enough to be born to relatively healthy parents? The first and most important characteristic experienced by the mentally sound child is his feeling, later a firm belief, that he is valued or loved. Feeling and believing that he is loved means that he has *value as a person.* A healthy parent or other primary caregivers have the capacity to communicate unconditional love and value to a child. They also have the ability to understand the necessity of separating the child's behavior from the child as a person. They know how to communicate unconditional love to the child while at the same time positively shaping his behavior. A less than mentally healthy or interpersonally inept adult is unable to understand this distinction or respond appropriately.

Consistently experiencing the feeling of being valued is the first element of positive self-concept development. To be most effective, understanding the child's perception at any given age is critical. The care giver's communication of unconditional love and value is perceived differently depending on the age of the child. For example, during the first eighteen months of life, the child does not psychologically experience himself as a separate entity from his caregivers. Consequently, every interaction, be it nonverbal, as in touching, or verbal, has an effect on the child's sense of self.

Later, with the acquisition of language, the child will be able to understand the meaning of words. Before language is learned, a parent's voice tone when responding is perceived by the infant or prelingual child as information about himself as a person. During this early developmental stage, the actual words used by the caregiver are not understood. What is heard, in the voice tone, are the emotions and attitude of the responder. An anxious or angry voice is incorporated by the infant as "bad me." The same is true nonverbally for the consistent absence of soothing physical touching. The infant or young child hears only the caregivers' feelings and what they do or not do behaviorally.

Starting at about eighteen to twenty-four months, the child

becomes increasingly aware that he is a separate entity from those around him. From this point on, the content of verbal responses and the emotions communicated by the caregiver become more and more discernable and therefore critical in the child's formation of their positive or negative primitive-self.

Without the child's conscious awareness, by the age of five, he has incorporated as truth much of what later can be identified as self-concept. A positive primitive-self is represented by a surface-self that is open and confident. The child demonstrates the ability to take risks in speaking and learning because he has confidence in himself and the courage to try new things. This positive sense of self, motivated by confidence and courage, is displayed at the verbal and behavioral levels. Another child of the same age with a negative self-concept would be hesitant to speak or act in a genuine manner, and have fear as a primary motivator for thinking and acting.

The mentally healthy child's confidence and courage will be demonstrated in everything from maintaining eye contact to the ease of verbal expression of feelings and thoughts. The secure child will be comfortable around strangers and able to easily socialize with peers. The young child will of course be alternately composed and confident and then be emotionally excessive. The difference is the child's openness and comfort in being honest about himself. It is always up to the parent to appropriately respond and shape the thinking, feeling, and behavior of the child. Every interaction is an opportunity for both to learn.

Mental Health: Age Seven to Eight Years

By the age of six or seven years, a child with a healthy self-concept is prepared for the cognitive developmental leap that occurs around this age. For the first time, the child becomes emotionally self-aware. He begins to have a primitive awareness of his thoughts and feelings, particularly those about himself. If the primitive-self has developed positively, the stage is set for continued healthful psychological development, the beginning emergence of the meta-self.

The child's surface-self, the part of the self seen and heard by others, becomes a reflection of a positive and confident primitive-self. The child will then begin the long process of successfully developing and incorporating a meta-self, his healthy adult self, as his mind's dominant feature. This process begins subtly in the young child and gradually accelerates and evolves throughout the individual's lifetime. The successful development of a meta-self, the mentally healthy adult self, is also dependent upon the development of cognitive abilities that enhance positive psychological growth. Of these capabilities, the conceptual ability of reasoned thinking is the most important.

A child with a positive self-concept feels free to express thoughts and feelings openly to others. His mentally healthy primary caregivers encourage the genuine expression of thought and feeling and help him to identify, understand, and evaluate the reasons that generate his emotions and thoughts. They teach the child how to both understand himself and appropriately express himself. Most importantly, they begin to respond in ways that stimulate and refine his conceptual abilities, especially the incorporation of reasoned thinking. This marks the beginning of *meta-self* development. For example, he begins to learn that he must manage his emotions. Are they valid? If so, how should they be expressed appropriately? He begins to realize that his feelings must not be the principle director for all his actions, but that he must filter them through reason-based thinking.

A mentally healthy child at the age of eight is beginning to understand and accept responsibility for the quality of his thinking and behavior. He is rapidly learning how to make responsible decisions, appropriately assert his rights, delay self-gratification, and be aware of and respond to the rights and needs of those around him. Remember, this learning is dependent on his caregivers understanding and modeling these healthful behaviors. No child lives and learns in a vacuum. Who we are and who we become is always primarily the product of the quality of our early social environment and how we as individuals perceive its messages.

Mental Health: Age Twelve to Fourteen

Preteens and younger teenagers, twelve to fourteen years old, are struggling with transitioning from being children, focused on enjoyable times with their parents and siblings, to understanding and meeting the challenges of the teen years. Chief among these challenges is an inner struggle to become independent and an outer struggle to relate successfully with people separate from the family, particularly their peers. Like most if not all teens, mentally healthy teens experience insecurity about themselves and their abilities. However, the mentally healthy teen is not ruled by momentary emotions, especially negative emotions. He has already learned to slow his thinking down when emotions rise, to allow reasoning to mediate his thinking. He is also able to share thoughts and feelings with people who are able to provide understanding and direction.

Most teenagers are vulnerable to peer pressure and the need to belong and be approved of by their peers. Mentally sound teenagers are no different except that they have limits to how far they will compromise in order to gain approval or acceptance. Psychologically they are further along than their peers in resolving the conflict between the power of peer influence over their thinking and behavior and the inner-reasoned thinking of their developing meta-self. To their peers they may be perceived as somewhat aloof or independent, and perhaps, a bit of a mystery.

The mentally healthy teenager will have varied interests. Those interests may involve activities at school with peers, or the activities may be separate from the usual pursuits of other teens. This is a reflection of a growing sense of psychological independence. Their self-concept will be challenged and shaped by their successes and failures during this period, but their inner ability to reason, coupled with a positive sense of self, will help them through the arduous psychological transition from child to young adult. Their primary motivator will be courage.

Mental Health: Age Seventeen or Eighteen

By the late teens, a positive self-concept is firmly established, and the cognitive development of the mind is well underway. Learning to use one's mind effectively is critical to the establishment of mental health and continued psychological growth. The development of reasoned thinking and objectivity enhance an already positive self-concept. The transition from emotion-based thinking to reason-based thinking is a gradual process. From a teaching standpoint, a dominant theme is encouraging the teenager to think for himself and learn to make choices that are responsible and contribute to his well-being. His self-efficacy is established because he is aware of and practices the principle of seeking truth through experience and reason-based thinking.

A mentally healthy aspiring adult of seventeen or eighteen is successfully tackling the challenges of transitioning from a teenager to an adult. Governed by a growing meta-self, the individual is by now developing a deeper sense of personal confidence, and responsibility, and concurrently the capacity for independence. The individual is learning to take responsibility for himself instead of being dependent on his family. He is also establishing psychological independence from peers and is beginning to assume control of the direction his life will take.

Mentally he is governed by reasoned thinking in the constructive management of his emotions. He is aware of the importance of emotions but also that the reasons behind the feelings are the source of truth and appropriate direction of his actions. He is learning to make informed decisions about himself and the world with a growing confidence in his mind's ability to know truth.

A mentally sound eighteen-year-old is beginning to demonstrate initiative and a sense of personal power and understanding in interpersonal relationships. Liking who he is as a person is a prerequisite to believing himself to be lovable. Having this positive sense of self provides a solid foundation for the young aspiring adult to make better choices in relationships. The healthy young person possesses the characteristics and skills that enhance the development and maintenance of nourishing relationships. In addition, he looks for and expects these healthful things to be given to him in return as he relates with others. His attitude about himself and his skill set are the basis for believing in and asserting his rights and needs in those relationships.

Along with the development of effective thinking abilities and a growing faith in these capabilities is the development of interpersonal competence in all types of relationships. He values and respects himself and has learned the importance of communicating respect to others. He values his ability to understand and empathically respond to others. He is also aware of the importance of communicating genuinely about himself and expecting others to be accountable for the same standard.

His well-developed positive self-concept provides a strong psychological foundation for being successful in setting and achieving personal goals. He believes in himself and has the courage necessary to face the challenges that adult life will present.

Mental Health: Age Thirty-Two to Thirty-Five, the Maturing Adult

The mentally healthy adult is always growing and changing in response to life's challenges. By the time a mentally sound individual reaches his thirties, he has a track record of dealing successfully with the challenges and responsibilities adult life brings. A lifelong positive, secure sense of self has facilitated success in all areas of life. When life presents problems, he has the internal psychological resources to explore, understand, and act effectively to solve them.

Learning to think with reasoning has solidified his confidence in his mind's ability to know truth. He is able to make decisions with confidence, solve problems, and plan programs to achieve goals that fulfill his needs. He has a positive attitude and a clear mind, and faith in himself to be able to achieve to the limit of his potential.

Having faith in oneself manifests in the individual's ability to feel confidence in any endeavor. He is primarily motivated by courage.

51

He is empowered by a set of conscious principles that guide his thinking and behavior. He is successful in relationships because he knows that he must give to other people what he expects to be given to him.

Because of his well-earned faith in himself and his ability to think with reasoning, he is psychologically independent. He trusts his judgment and changes what he believes as new learning is assimilated. The mentally sound individual listens well to others but accepts what they have to say as truth only if it makes better sense than he has made to himself. He is independent and even single-minded, and yet he is able to relate to others empathically and with additive understanding.

The mentally healthy adult faces life's challenges knowing that with knowledge and hard work he can understand and accomplish almost anything he sets his mind to do. He accepts that he will make mistakes in thinking and behaving, but he is confident that he has the ability to learn from those mistakes.

People who have been fortunate enough to develop and experience psychological quality as a constant in their lives know the importance of valuing one's self as a person. They understand that valuing one's self is the prerequisite for being able to love others and for believing they are worthy of being loved. Because they believe in their value as a person, they learn to believe in their right and responsibility to think for themselves. They learn through trial and error that thinking for themselves provides the necessary psychological foundation for learning to trust their judgment and for building trust and the ability of their own minds to discern truth. Because they have faith in their minds, they have faith in themselves.

Individuals with a strong positive self-concept have learned to not accept what they have been taught in the past as truth without regard for its validity and applied functionality. They accept only truth that is based on the acceptance of reality and examined by their own reasoned thinking. Finally, they own that it is their responsibility to shape their present and future experience for the better. In that endeavor, their belief in themselves allows them to be their own best ally and advocate. *They have reached a higher level of self-satisfaction, psychological independence, and personal psychological responsibility that is the exception in societies, not the rule.* They experience true mental health. They live *psychological quality.*

Androgynous Mental Health

Is the type or form of mental health different for men and women? No. The fundamental elements of psychological health are androgynous. This fact is true not only for gender but also for race, nationality, culture, or time. With that said, there are a few general differences between the *learned* nature and behavior of the genders. These differences are reflected in the attitudes and behaviors of men and women.

As little girls, women are taught to be more relationship focused than boys. They are taught to empathize with and take care of people they are close to. Consequently, women are more responsive, agreeable, and compliant in relationships. Women are taught as little girls that taking care of others is their responsibility and that in return their needs will be met by those they take care of. Getting along with others is a priority. Acknowledging and caring about the feelings of others is also a learned priority for women.

Early childhood learning for boys focuses not on relationship building but rather on self-sufficiency, risk taking, problem solving, and goal achievement. They are taught to compete with other boys and that winning is always the goal. Boys are taught to solve problems on their own by thinking for themselves. Emotionally they are taught to minimize their feelings and that the expression of feelings is a weakness, therefore feelings are repressed or minimized. Further, boys are taught aggression as a primary solution instead of using reasoning, empathy, and compromise to resolve conflicts. Too many are also taught to avoid taking responsibility for being wrong.

Regardless of gender, the characteristics that represent mental health are the same. These androgynous factors include the psychological and interpersonal strengths that are displayed by either gender. For example, the woman's caring and giving attitude, sensitivity, and empathic skills and the man's self-assured attitude, assertiveness, and motivation for achievement professionally are all admirable beneficial characteristics and indicative of mental health.

Now that the reader has a sample of what mental health looks like at various stages of life, I will introduce in subsequent chapters a more in-depth examination of specific mental health elements and interpersonal competencies. Additionally, I will discuss the range of these elements from the lowest level of pathological impairment to the highest level of mental health and interpersonal efficacy. In addition, I will discuss the interrelationship of the various elements and competencies.

4

Self-Concept and Mental Health

Valuing the Self

The concept of valuing the psychological self is historically a fairly recent idea that has its roots in Western Europe during the period of history known as the Renaissance. Valuing the *individual self* is the philosophical position maintaining that a single person, in contrast to the group, is of inherent value and should be treated justly and with respect. Additionally, each individual possesses the right of self-determination and the right and responsibility to think, feel, and act in a manner that is in his own best interest. America was founded upon this principle of the inherent right of the individual, but because man lives in groups, this responsibility extends to the best interest of others.

The advent and study of the *psychological* self as a concept began with the foundation of psychology in the late 1800s. In psychology, the notion of the *self* refers to a person's experience as a single, unitary, autonomous being that is separate from others and experienced with continuity through time and place. The experience of the self includes consciousness of one's physical self as well as one's inner character and emotional life.

More recent perceptions concerning the self usually are limited to brief discussions that point out the value of self-esteem to having a fulfilling life. In the psychological literature, the self has many meanings, which can be characterized as diverse, superficial, contradictory, and confusing, both to professionals in the field and to the general public. Understanding the practical importance of the self, and in particular the self-concept, with regard to mental health and mental illness, ranges from nonexistent to token reference as a symptom of some psychological disorders. A negative self-concept, and the destructive power it can have as a cause of mental illness, or a myriad of subclinical mental and interpersonal issues, is not even considered a diagnosable disorder.

The consequence of man's pervasive negative sense of self is that it causes the individual to become mentally separated from his real self. He represses the truth about what and how he actually believes about himself. To nourish his pervasive anxiety and escape from himself, he becomes focused on external self-interest and particularly short-term self-gratification to avoid conscious awareness of his negative beliefs. Blocking knowledge of the real self results in partial or complete lack of self-awareness, self-understanding, and self-nourishment. Over time self-concept erodes and psychological growth is limited or halted and deterioration begins.

As human beings, we all share two fundamental but profound psychological needs throughout our lives. We all want and need a positive self-concept, to value who we are as a person, and we want to experience nourishing, fulfilling, and intimate relationships with others. We want to genuinely like and love ourselves and love others and be loved in return.

People who live with poor perceptions of themselves are unable to adequately meet these needs, even though they spend their entire lives attempting to do so, to the best of their ability. The reason they are unsuccessful is that they are either educationally or psychologically impaired. Regardless of the reasons for their deficits, the result of their impairment is that they have a *negative self-concept.*

Having a negative self-concept means a life filled with disappointment, discouragement, and despair. It also means people live life dominated by fear. A person motivated by fear is at best defensive, evasive, cognitively and emotionally limited, and self-defeating. Depending on the degree of dysfunctionality, fear is experienced either consciously or subconsciously. It becomes the primary motivator in their lives, determining everything they do or don't do. In the most severe cases, a negative self-concept and its constant companion, fear, mean a lifetime of psychological isolation from people's real selves and from others. It can also mean a lifetime of needing to escape from one's self through adopting an addictive behavior as a solution to the negative self-awareness.

Erich Fromm, in *Man for Himself*, concluded that modern man's problems with his self is not that he is too self-centered or self-indulgent. It is rather that he does not have the ability to love himself.[1] Man does not love himself because he does not like, respect, or value who he is and how he lives his life. Having a negative self-concept is a pervasive problem for man, and it affects the majority of people. Too many people "lead lives of quiet desperation."[2] I contend that man needs to be more concerned with the quality of the relationship he has with himself and learn that he has the responsibility and the power to change that relationship for the better. He need not settle for what he was taught to believe about himself if it has caused his life to be a constant negative experience.

It seems obvious that the lucky people who enjoy a genuinely *positive self-concept* are more likely to be mentally healthy. They are also more likely to be effective in establishing and maintaining healthful, nourishing, and therefore fulfilling relationships. Those who possess a positive relationship with themselves and are mentally healthy have faith in themselves and the confidence it engenders. They trust in the efficacy of their minds. They are motivated by courage to achieve to the limit of their individual potential and are accordingly able to genuinely enjoy all that the great gift of life has to offer.

---

1   Erich Fromm, *Man for Himself: An Inquiry into the Psychology of Ethics* (New York: Holt, Reinhart & Winston, 1947).
2   Henry D. Thoreau, *Walden*, ed. J. Lyndon Shanley (Princeton, NJ: Princeton University press, 1971), 8.

Self-Concept Defined

The self is a psychological term referring to the structure of a person's subjective experience of himself. The self-concept is comprised of what the individual believes as truth about himself, his actual thoughts and feelings about himself—his quality as a person, his quality in relation to others, and his potential for achieving in the outside world.

In the most general sense, the *self*'s purposes are directed toward the mastery of reality and reality tasks through organizing experience in a manner that makes sense out of both the outside world *and itself*. In turn, the self's organization of experience provides the perceptual basis for the development of the individual's self-concept.

The individual's self-concept takes the content form of beliefs, feelings, attitudes, and values. This subjective content is, for better or worse, a product of the individual's early life experience and the quality of his thinking. Beliefs are *subjective* cognitive conclusions concerning what is *personally* thought to be real and true about one's self and the world. The earliest and deepest set of beliefs are *core beliefs* about the self. Once formed, these personal and powerful core beliefs are accepted as reality and guide all further perceptions, inquiries, and conclusions for that individual. All subsequent action by the individual is affected, if not driven, by the content and quality of his self-concept. The self-concept, the subjectively constructed reality, directs the course and quality of an individual's life—*for better or worse*.

Individuals with a negative self-concept of a subclinical or clinical nature have developed an internal belief structure that is, to some degree, irrational, harmful, and destructive to themselves and usually others around them. An individual may be aware of his negative beliefs about himself but conclude that his perceived reality is normal and therefore healthy. (In psychological parlance, "normal" means "typical," not "mentally healthy"). He may live his entire life secretly feeling bad about who he is as a person without realizing the harm it does to himself and others. Or the person may be aware of his negative sense of self, and its consequences in his life, but feel powerless to change. A negative self-concept is at the base of most forms of mental illness. Subclinically, a negative sense of self and its consequences are central features of most unhappy and unfulfilled lives.

To remain constantly conscious of one's real self, when the perception is primarily negative, is an unpleasant experience, to say the least. To face and own one's negative self-perception and its harmful consequences is an arduous mental task. It is much easier to rationalize one's experience and externalize blame to something or someone else. Owning responsibility for being the cause of your psychological impairment is the first step in changing yourself and your life for the better. To undertake real self-change takes courage and commitment.

Elements that Define Self-Concept

"Self-concept" is the comprehensive term that encompasses other characteristics, including *self-esteem, self-efficacy, self-respect, self-confidence,* and *self-advocacy.* At this point an explanation of these terms is appropriate for clarification.

Self-esteem is the subjectively perceived amount of worth or value individuals attribute to themselves. Does the individual see himself as lovable, competent, and deserving? The existing level of perceived self-esteem is the most critical variable in determining overall self-concept. A low level of self-esteem means that the individual perceives a low sense of personal value and therefore is not deserving of happiness, love, or achievement.

Self-efficacy concerns an individual's ability to trust his own mental thought processes. A high sense of self-efficacy enables one to trust his mind to make independent and accurate judgments about himself and the world. To possess self-efficacy is to trust both the validity of one's beliefs and to have confidence in the mental process capabilities of one's mind.

Self-respect is to like what one sees as the truth about oneself. It is the feeling of confidence and pride in your own self-worth and competence. It is the belief that one has equal value as a person to anyone else and therefore deserves to be treated accordingly. It is also the belief that one has rights in relationships and the right to assert one's self to obtain them. Finally, self-respect is demonstrated in the degree of ethical and moral quality one chooses to live.

Self-confidence is the pride and self-assurance a person feels about himself—the knowledge that he has the ability to use his mind to understand and to do things competently. In addition, self-confidence can be situation or skill specific in that it is the result of demonstrated ability to do a specific activity well. For example, he may have self-confidence in his professional life yet lack self-confidence in his personal life.

Self-advocacy is the practice of being one's own best ally in one's mind, and in any endeavor.

Self-Concept, the product of these characteristics combined, is the most important element in determining the development and conservation of mental health.

Expressions of Positive Self-Concept and Its Major Components

Self-esteem is the most significant component of an individual's overall self-concept. According to Nathaniel Branden, self-esteem is the belief that one is worthy of living and competent to do so successfully.[3] A person's subjectively perceived level of self-esteem determines what an individual sees as possible for him to expect or achieve in life. Low self-esteem inhibits successful psychological maturation, interpersonal relating (especially intimacy), and learning of all types.

Self-esteem, self-efficacy, self-respect, self-confidence, and self-advocacy as elements of a positive self-concept are evident in one's attitude toward oneself and about life. I have combined my thoughts with Nathaniel Branden's as to how a positive self-concept and high self-esteem are expressed. Common forms of expression include:

---

3   Nathaniel Branden, *The Psychology of Self-Esteem* (Los Angeles: Nash Publishing, 1969).

- a manner and way of talking and moving that projects the pleasure one takes in being alive and being who one is;

- an ease in talking of accomplishments or shortcomings with directness and honesty;

- the comfort one experiences in giving and receiving compliments, expressions of affection, or appreciation;

- an openness to criticism and a comfort about acknowledging mistakes because one's self-esteem is not tied to an image of "being perfect";

- one's words and movements having a quality of ease and spontaneity, reflecting the fact that one is not at war with one's self;

- the congruence between what one says and does and how one looks, sounds, and moves;

- an attitude of openness to and curiosity about new ideas, new experiences, and new possibilities of life;

- the fact that feelings of anxiety or insecurity, if they appear, will be less likely to intimidate or overwhelm since accepting them, managing them, and rising above them rarely feels impossibly difficult;

- the ability to enjoy the humorous aspects of life in oneself and others;

- a flexibility in responding to situations and challenges since one trusts one's mind and does not see life as doom or defeat;

- a comfort with assertive (not belligerent) behavior in oneself and others; and

- the ability to preserve a quality of harmony and dignity under conditions of stress.

The human experience of a highly positive self-concept is the exception, not the rule. Because self-efficacy, self-respect, self-confidence, and self-advocacy are subsets of self-concept, observing them at high levels is equally as rare. Unfortunately, more than half of all people live with a negative sense of self that is to varying degrees detrimental in their lives.

People at the most severe levels of impairment are so psychologically alienated and isolated from *themselves* that their negative self-attitude and its consequences are largely, if not completely, unknown to them. Those with partial self-awareness of their condition engage in constant and varied distractions to distance themselves from the negative experience of contact with their real selves. Many of these individuals practice various forms of denial as self-defense mechanisms. Many others choose escape from themselves through addictive behavior, which helps them to avoid lucid moments of self-deprecation and conscious suffering. They deny the reality that the addiction is not a viable solution. In fact, addiction hastens the destruction of themselves and their relationships with others.

A Continuum of Self-Esteem Functioning

The level or quality of an individual's self-esteem is expressed overtly in observed attitude and behavior. The following is an attitude and behavior description of the five levels of observable behavior that reflect the range of expressed self-esteem from the lowest level of self-regard to the highest level of constructive self-valuing.

Level 1: Primitive-Self: Dysfunctional

At this lowest level of functioning, the individual has a predominantly negative opinion of himself but is unaware of his real beliefs and feelings. To the objective observer, the individual is quick to blame others instead of taking responsibility and is unaware or unconcerned about how his own actions adversely affect him or those with whom he interacts. His spoken words often contradict observed feelings and behavior. The primary emotional states observed include anger, fear, helplessness, and/or confusion.

Level 2: Primitive-Self: Dysfunctional

At this level the individual has a limited emotional self-awareness and a poor self-concept. This condition may be owned to some degree. Significant areas of irrational or destructive behavior are unknown or rationalized. Low self-esteem is more likely to be owned than at the lowest level, but little is done to understand or act responsibly to improve this condition. If this person does take any responsibility, it is vague, confused, and inconsistent in occurrence. Blaming others and sometimes oneself is a common part of this person's life.

Level 3: Mixed Primitive- and Meta-Self

The Level 3 person is consciously self-aware and at least somewhat aware and concerned about others. Self-esteem is generally positive but blind spots are evident. Blind spots are areas of negative unknown that are reflected in displays of poor self-esteem, helplessness, immaturity, or aggressive behavior and difficulty in interpersonal relationships. The individual is either unaware the effect his adverse behavior has on others or he misinterprets their responses. Outside help is required to uncover hidden beliefs that reflect a negative self-concept and the resulting negative consequences.

Level 4: Above-Average Meta-Self Functioning

The Level 4 individual displays a consistently high positive and valid level of self-esteem. This positive self-esteem enables an above-average perceptive ability of others because he is not distracted by overfocusing on himself. At this level an individual has a high degree of self-efficacy and the ability to be rationally assertive. The individual is able to be productive, helpful, and additive in relationships. Because he trusts his own mind, he is able to solve problems in all areas of living. The individual is an initiator and manages successful life changes with minimum outside direction. Interpersonally the individual is experienced by others as being self-assured and confident.

Level 5: Highest Level of Meta-Self Functioning

At this highest level of functioning, the individual possesses a consistently strong positive sense of self-esteem, a high degree of psychological self-integration, and autonomy. Self-integration means that the individual is one person psychologically. The person that he is inside with himself is the same person that he relates with to the outside world. Additionally, conceptual awareness and objectivity and interpersonal genuineness are all present at high levels. The individual is consciously aware of his innermost thoughts and feelings because of a high degree of self-objectivity. Additional character traits include a high degree of integrity and interpersonal effectiveness in all situations. These competencies are demonstrated along with a high empathic regard for the feelings and rights of others. Finally, this individual is one who encourages and teaches others to live in a positive self-affirming and productive manner.

In Summary

The quality of an individual's self-concept, for better or worse, determines that individual's destiny. A positive self-concept opens the door to all possibilities within the range of a person's effort and talents. However, a negative self-concept, evident in over half of the population, leads to a lifetime of low expectations, underachievement, troubled and failed relationships, loss of faith in one's self, and eventually self-destruction.

5

The Creation of the Self and Early Psychological Development

Inherited and Learned Traits

Every person begins life with an *inherited* genetic set of physical attributes, intellectual abilities, and psychological characteristics. Inherited factors are elements such as physical size, skin color, the presence of certain mental or physical deficits or diseases, special talents, psychological temperament, intellectual intelligence potential, and also, I believe, a range of potential for psychological intelligence, reasoning ability, and mental health. These genetic factors and others form man's inherited hardware that give direction and help determine his future development. It is generally accepted in the professional literature that 20 percent of who we become is controlled by genetic factors. The other 80 percent is determined by what happens to us after we are born.

On the inherited side, for example, an individual is born with a given temperament (psychological disposition) that can be placed somewhere along a passive/aggressive psychological continuum:

Passive/Reserved--------------Assertive--------------------Aggressive

Well-known observable examples are the extremely shy child who reflects the passive end of the continuum, contrasted by the overly aggressive child at the other end. If the placement on the continuum is to the extreme on either the passive or aggressive end, psychological and interpersonal problems to some degree will be a probability. If the excessively passive or aggressive person is not constructively shaped to the extent possible during childhood and adolescent development, extreme temperament will, to some degree, adversely affect perception, thinking ability, interpersonal relating, and consequently self-concept, mental health, and psychological fulfillment in general. For healthy psychological self-development, both cases of extreme temperament need increased amounts of understanding and guidance from primary and secondary caregivers during the formative years of development.

The other major factors that do the most to determine who we are and who we can become are the products of our experiences after we are born and our learned way of perceiving those experiences. Psychologically, the most basic and powerful things we learn early in childhood are the beliefs we form about ourselves. These are the core beliefs that define what we believe as absolute truth about ourselves and, by extension, what is possible for us to experience or achieve in life. These beliefs may or may not be true when held up to reality, but if the individual *believes* them, then those beliefs are truth to him.

Once we accept a set of facts, rational or irrational, about ourselves as truth, we can become psychologically entrapped by those beliefs for life, especially if they are negative. All subsequent thinking is based on perceptions from within that box of learned accepted truths. This box defines both our perception of reality and our personal identity. Generally, the only thing that will challenge our early learned truth is the experience of a major life crisis. In this case, change is forced on the individual either by an outside agent or by an important decision that the individual must make. An example of an outside agent that causes crisis is a hurricane. An important life decision would be the choice to get a divorce.

The Brain and the Mind

Acquiring an understanding about the elements that constitute mental health must also include essential information concerning the nature and workings of the mind.

The human brain is the physical object in which the mind exists. However, unlike the brain, the human *mind* is not a physical object. It is rather the intellectual and psychological "content" of the brain— the data, the thoughts and feelings it creates. A comparison with a computer is a good analogy. The computer, its component parts, are the computer's brain. The software, the programs put into the computer, are the computer's mind. They use the physical system of the computer to complete processes for chosen tasks.

One's mind is always in a state of activity at both conscious and subconscious levels. A mind is constantly perceiving, ordering, and choosing among all the information it takes in in order to perform a multitude of specific mental and behavioral tasks. The overall purpose of one's mind is to make sense out of the individual's experience of himself and the world around him and to help him function effectively in his environment. The mind's content is a collection of *subjectively perceived and processed* information that develops in the form of mental habits, abilities, and beliefs that portend to provide understanding and meaning for its proprietor.

In learning about the processes of the mind, the most relevant fact to the reader is that the mental operations of perceiving, ordering, and in general just making sense out of observed facts is a *learned subjective thinking process*—not an objective process. It's probably obvious to the reader that people do not perceive or interpret actions or events in the same way or with the same level of quality. Researchers have documented that people often view an event differently, and that they draw different conclusions and meanings from the same event. This is because perceiving, interpreting, and attributing meaning to anything is influenced by the *biased thinking and uniqueness of each person*. Individual experience, attitude, temperament, intelligence (intellectual and psychological), environmental influences, and even emotional mood are among the causes of variance in both how and what people perceive. Most important is that everything is filtered through the subjective core beliefs the individual holds about himself and the outside world.

Obviously then, since we all process and arrive at perceived truth subjectively, it is again the *quality of one's subjective thinking* that is important—the quality of mental processes and the resulting content. A young child is unable to choose how his primitive-self is formed. However, once reaching chronological adulthood, it is the individual's responsibility to assess the health and quality of his mind's content, processes, and conclusions. This is especially important in regard to the beliefs he has formed about himself—his self-concept.

Early Formation of the Self

From a developmental standpoint, an individual's mental self and the content of his mind can be divided into three interrelated psychological components: *primitive-self, surface-self, and meta-self.*

The *primitive-self* is the portion of your mind that is formed earliest in life. It is shaped during the first six years of life. It is therefore your child self, with only a child's emotion-centered perceptual ability. Once formed, the primitive-self becomes the foundation upon which the other features of one's self are built. The quality of the primitive-self, its level of mental soundness, determines the course and quality of the other facets of one's self—the surface-self and the meta-self.

The *surface-self* is the portion of one's mind that is presented to and interacts with the outside world. In early childhood before the age of six, if self-development is positive, the surface-self is an open reflection of the primitive-self. This is true only if the primitive-self is positive. If the primitive-self is formed with a negative valence, the surface-self is not a genuine reflection of the primitive-self. Instead, the surface-self gradually and subconsciously becomes a protective mask of the negative self.

Around the age of six, a child gains a conscious, rudimentary emotional awareness of his self for the first time. If his self-awareness experience is troubling, the surface-self will continue its development as a protective agent in collusion with the *troubled primitive-self.* Its primary focus will be to hide the troubled self from the outside world *and from the child's own conscious awareness.* In addition to shielding the child from its negative beliefs and feelings about itself, the surface-self's outward goal will be to do what it has to for survival in its social environment.

Blocking self-awareness to survive comes at a high psychological cost. The child learns to block its conscious awareness of its true thoughts and feelings. Loss of contact with feelings and proceeding thoughts ensures the lack of conscious connection with the real primitive-self and ensures the limiting or blocking of continued self-development toward psychological health throughout both childhood and adulthood.

If the child's primitive-self development is positive, his psychological development will proceed in a healthier direction. The surface-self will accurately represent the healthy primitive-self. As the child matures toward adulthood, a healthy meta-self will gradually be formed and the surface-self will become the representative of the meta-self. It will accurately reflect the meta-self and effectively perform its function to interact in healthful ways with the outside world.

The *meta-self* is the rational, healthy, competent, responsible, and eventually mature facet of one's mind. The meta-self's development begins as a small part of a healthy primitive-self, but, as one matures psychologically, it gradually takes over as governor of all thinking, feeling, and behavioral processes. Given that healthy psychological development occurs, by chronological adulthood the meta-self is well seated as the dominant portion of one's mind. The meta-self will continue its development and refinement throughout adult life.

The Development of Mental Health in Infancy and Early Childhood

I have value as a person, and therefore I am worthy of being loved.
As introduced above, development of one's mind and the psy-

chological self happens in stages. The first stage of self-development is the forming of the primitive-self. Emergence of the primitive-self begins most likely when a child is in a fetal state. A child in the womb of its mother is subject to many factors that may contribute to self-development. The most important of these may be the mother's psychological health and the effect of her emotional states on the developing fetus. However, at the present time there is little scientific evidence to confirm this possibility or other influences that may be present in utero.

Developmental factors that are supported by science and common sense include both genetically inherited physical, intellectual, and psychological traits. The mother's physical health, nutritional habits, and drug usage are elements that can affect the fetus and developing young child. Other inherited traits include potential for intelligence, both psychological and intellectual, temperament (passive to aggressive behavioral tendencies), physical abilities, and special talents.

From the moment of birth, the mother's mental health and the quality of her every interaction with the infant has an effect for better or worse on the formation of the infant's psychological self. Clinically this concept is called "stage appropriate empathic responding." The nature and quality of one's primitive-self is a product of the child's collective interactive experience with all significant others during the first few years of life.

To sum up, one's primitive sense of self consists of a blending of inherited traits or characteristics determined before birth and by the quality of interactions experienced with primary caregivers during the early years of life. Inherited traits can be enhanced or limited by the quality of the primary social interactions experienced. Therefore, the quality of parenting (primary caregiving) is crucial in the development of a healthy sense of self. Parents or other caregivers who are themselves psychologically healthy and interpersonally competent are much more likely to raise psychologically/emotionally healthy children.

Primary caregivers who are psychologically impaired are destined to have a negative influence on a developing child. For example, how could a parent teach a child to have a positive sense of self (self-concept) if he does not have one himself? Or how could a parent instill the values and skills of reasoned thinking if he lacks the ability to reason? How can he teach a child to be honest if he is not honest? During the first few years of life, children learn primarily from what their caregivers do (model), not what they say. In fact, young children hear primarily two things in their interactions with others. They hear the other's emotions as they are expressed nonverbally, during the prelingual period, and once language is acquired, the actual feeling words. The other things all children can hear is what the other person actually does behaviorally. Young children are especially attuned to expressed emotions, which are always perceived by a child as being about him.

Through gradual experiencing, in a psychologically healthful social environment, the evolving self constructively shapes itself and its perception of the world. The child develops a primitive-self that has a positive set of self-beliefs and a basic functional working knowledge of internal and external reality. Consequently, during the various stages of future psychological development, the child is able to successfully meet early life challenges. He feels good about who he is, knows right from wrong, and is learning to trust his mind to know how to solve the ever-present challenges that life presents. In contrast, a child with a psychologically troubled primitive-self, to varying degrees, will experience difficulty in effectively responding to normal developmental challenges.

When a child's early psychological environment is as it should be, psychological development of the primitive-self proceeds according to the natural characteristics found in the positive nature of man. The child reared in a psychologically nourishing environment, where effective parental figures are present, will develop a primitive-self that includes a positive secure perception of self. For example, effective parents know the importance of separating the child, as a person, from the child's behavior. They understand that valuing their child, as a person, is demonstrated by the communication of unconditional love for the person in spite of its behavior. They know that the child's feelings are simply information about his emotional state and that his behavior is only an expression of his thoughts and feelings. They are separate from his quality as a person. He is not a bad person just because he is angry or misbehaves. He is not a good person just because he is doing what his parents want him to do.

Effective parents consistently communicate the child's value as a person while they respond appropriately to shape both his self-concept and his behavior. In a healthy home, a child experiences being valued as a person and learns how to perceive, manage, and express himself positively and appropriately. Because the child can trust his parents, valuing of him, he will also develop trust in himself and his own growing mental abilities.

Because of yet undeveloped cognitive abilities and the dominance of the primitive-self, a child in the first few years of life is driven primarily by immediate thoughts and feelings. As the child develops cognitively, his thoughts, feelings, and behavior become more and more ordered and complex. If the primary caregivers are able to respond appropriately to successive stages of the child's emotional and cognitive development, then the child will continue to build upon a positive set of beliefs about himself and his abilities.

With the consistent experience of feeling valued, the child will in time believe in his right to be valued by others because he believes in his own worth. The belief of having and deserving value is a fundamental, critical building block of a positive self-concept *and becomes the foundation for all future beneficial psychological development.*

The experience of feeling valued and believing one has the *right* to be valued is also the beginning of believing one's self to be worthy of being loved by others. Having one's thoughts and feelings about one's self positively validated sets the stage for trusting one's mind to function effectively (self-efficacy). So, being valued and feeling valuable sparks faith in one's mind and in one's self.

The Power of Early Learned Beliefs

The developing child's learned primitive self-concept defines his perception of reality—the truth about who he is and who he can be. Thus created, these personal beliefs determine the positive or negative characteristics a person sees in himself. This set of personal core beliefs is composed of many thoughts and feelings organized into dominant beliefs about himself and the world. They define not only the perceived truth about his value as a person but also his perceived potential for all that life offers.

An individual's subjective self-beliefs can be positive, productive, and beneficial to him and others, or they may be negative, limiting, and destructive to himself and others with whom he comes in contact. Following are questions about one's self that are consciously or subconsciously answered *for better or worse* by every individual at a young age and repeatedly throughout life:

- Am I a person of value — as much value as any other person?

- Am I deserving of love?

- How intelligent am I?

- In what areas am I gifted or talented?

- In what areas am I not so bright?

- Am I an emotionally strong person?

- Do my emotional and actual ages match?

- Do others like me?

- What do I fear?

- Am I a risk taker?

- How attractive am I?

- Do I relate well with others?

- Do I stand up for myself when I need to?

- Can I make good decisions without help from others?

- Am I competent in one or more areas of potential achievement?

- Can I trust my thinking processes?

- What is my attitude about life in general?

It is these personal beliefs—the subjective content of one's mind—that determines the actual quality of existence, achievement, and fulfillment experienced by each of us. Once answered and accepted as truth, these beliefs form the individual's self-identity for better or worse. *Subsequent thinking and resulting behavior will seek to reinforce and confirm one's perceived identity—especially if the beliefs about self are negative.*

When the primitive-self gets an appropriate nurturing beginning, the stage is set for healthy development of the individual's surface-self and later the meta-self. More specifically, a positive primitive-self—being in touch with one's real self, feeling safe, feeling valued, and trusting in one's mind—forms the necessary foundation for creation and constructive growth of a meta-self. If all goes well, by the time a child reaches chronological adulthood, the meta-self will be well under way to assuming constructive control of all thinking and behaving.

In Summary

It is generally accepted knowledge that intellectually we learn half of all we know in the first year of life. I believe this is true for the intellectual domain of learning. However, in the psychological domain, learning is a more gradual process of experience, perception, and acquired knowledge. Each individual creates a self-concept based on the quality of his environment in early childhood, and to a lesser extent, his inherited traits and talents. A major mental product of this process is the construction of personal beliefs. The most important of these beliefs are those we create as truth about ourselves.

We are all, to varying degrees, products of what we learn as truth about the world and ourselves in the first few years of life. Our existence and our identities are intertwined with this early learning. Because a negative self-concept is learned, it is also possible that it can be unlearned and replaced by a positive self-concept. Once becoming an adult, an individual has the responsibility to identify, challenge, and unlearn faulty and perhaps destructive beliefs about himself. He can then construct a mentally sound self-concept composed of healthful beliefs about himself that are based on reality and reasoned thinking.

New learning, which seeks to alter those limiting and harmful core beliefs, requires thinking outside of the current conceptual box. It entails opening one's mind to ideas that challenge early learned truths. This ability is difficult for most of us and impossible for many. A great deal of determination and perhaps some outside objective help may be necessary.

The elements of a positive self-concept can and should become a fundamental part of preventive education for schoolchildren. Adults, especially perspective and actual parents, could be taught the tenets of positive beliefs about oneself and the importance of their own self-concept in facilitating the fostering of a positive sense of self in their children. A person cannot give a gift that he does not possess.

6

The Myth of Adulthood

Regardless of what is genetically inherited or learned in childhood, the adult individual has the sole responsibility of choosing the course and quality of his life. As individuals we have the ability to change because we are primarily the developmental product of noninherited environmental factors. As much as 80 percent of who we become is learned and therefore can be unlearned. These are the factors of environment and experience that affect most of our early physical, intellectual, and especially our psychological learning. Noninherited factors form man's cognitive and emotional software (learned beliefs and responses) and interact with inherited factors to determine who he ultimately becomes.

To achieve psychological quality, it will be necessary to unlearn much of what we were taught as truth early in life about the world and especially ourselves. Learned negative beliefs about ourselves, biases, and dysfunctional behaviors must be unlearned and replaced by rational, valid, and beneficial beliefs and behaviors. Through patience, hard work, and new knowledge, every individual has the choice and ability to shape and develop his future psychological life in a more positive and beneficial direction. Depending on the degree of impairment and the amount of inner resistance to change, the guidance of a helping professional may be needed to facilitate the self-change process.

Along with establishing an atmosphere of trust, a counselor's first major treatment goal in cases involving negative sense of self must be to put the individual in touch with his true perceptions of himself and the world. Conscious awareness of one's core or innermost beliefs about himself is the beginning of real change toward mental health. An individual's core beliefs, especially the negative ones, must be revealed in order to be changed. If the individual does not know the content of subconscious core beliefs that determine the content and processes of ones thinking and feeling, he cannot change them. These hidden beliefs must be made conscious to be evaluated for rationality, validity, and beneficiality. If negative self-beliefs are valid, then constructive change can be initiated. If the negative beliefs are erroneous or irrational, they can be rejected and replaced by new valid beliefs that are reality based.

If an individual's self-concept is negative, there is a corresponding lack of faith in his self. His believed unworthiness will be evident in a lack of sufficient faith in his ability to think clearly and decisively. He is likely to be overly dependent on others to confirm his thinking and acting. Additionally, a negative self-concept means that he will perceive most of what he thinks and does is wrong or substandard. He will also doubt his ability to know anything for sure.

In cases where dysfunctionality is greater, the individual will cut off conscious awareness of his negative self-concept. Separating from conscious awareness of negative self-thoughts is subconsciously invoked early in life as a self-protective solution, but it is a solution that only exacerbates the problem. Regardless of the level of self-awareness or the veracity of the particular beliefs concerning the self, beliefs are accepted subconsciously as reality by the individual. The erroneous beliefs are repeatedly and unwittingly verified through self-structured failure. A negative self-fulfilling prophecy is established as a psychological lifestyle. The continued nourishment of a poor self-concept becomes a destructive cycle that is increasingly debilitating as life unfolds.

Simply stated, we *are* what we think. What we believe consciously and subconsciously about ourselves, for better or for worse, is accepted as the truth. Our internal self beliefs and our beliefs about the world define our individual perception of reality—the reality of who we are and what is real and possible for us in life. An individual's belief structure is for better or worse—true or false, rational or irrational, healthy or pathological, constructive or destructive.

Psychological Immaturity as Pathology

Let's begin with an unsettling fact. The psychological age of the average adult is sixteen years. This means that the average adult functions as an adolescent. If that fact seems difficult to believe, take a few moments to consider:

- the target psychological age level of most television shows. Too many are replete with mindless adolescent humor, poor grammar, crude and crud language, sexual innuendo, and violence. The content of video games is much worse in condoning violence. Psychologically, people have learned that violence is fun. Only the mentally sound individual knows the difference between fantasy programs via the media and real life, and they are the minority.

- the adolescent gullibility of viewers who allow the biased media to reinforce their black-and-white unreasoned opinions. The media offers networks that pander to any belief or value structure. Most networks target certain segments of population and provide false, exaggerated, and biased programing that keeps their viewers watching.

- the adolescent perception of political corruption. Dishonesty in politics is accepted as the norm or a necessary evil. Power, money, and fame are goals for most politicians. Too many people know that politicians are in it for themselves and yet fail to do anything about it. These same people feel powerless to do something to change a system that is dysfunctional most of the time and works against the best interest of the majority. Public figures model philosophical extremism on both sides, and this is seen as acceptable for individuals, especially ones with adolescent perceptions and values. Political polarization is now our norm for political involvement, including the right to hate the opposition. Nothing good will come of holding on to this political belief structure.

- the wavering but still strong adolescent belief that religion or god is going to do anything to make this world better. Man's inhumanity to man is readily apparent throughout history and alive and well in the tenants and behavior of all religions today. Why does man refuse to see religion for what it is and isn't? Man makes his own problems and must also solve them. No mythical belief, festooned with ritualistic traditions, empty promises, and fear-engendering dogma is going to solve anything. Traditional religion, regardless of its professed good values, divides us and contributes to our mistaken beliefs about ourselves and others.

It is a well known and unfortunately widely accepted fact that children mature more slowly now than they did fifty years ago. More young adults are living with their parents, or are living separately but still psychologically dependent on their parents, well into their twenties and early thirties and beyond. Parents rationalize their children's behavior to make it acceptable, and they are unable or unwilling to require them to leave or become independent. Too many parents use their adult children's dependence for their own mistaken psychological purposes. These adult children do not have to grow up and be responsible for themselves, and many are too immature to know how.

Let's look at a typical case. A few years ago, I interviewed a prospective patient who claimed she needed counseling to get enough courage to leave her husband of thirty-five years. She stated that all they did was fight and coexist with great emotional distance between them. My first suggestion was to invite her husband into a counseling session. My overall intention or goal was to save the marriage if possible. My short-term goal was to identify the real problem. When the husband came in, I asked both of them what they fight about that keeps them at odds. The answer turned out to be constant arguments about their son.

The son was twenty-five years old and still living at home. He had part-time jobs periodically. In listening to each of their perceptions about their relationships with their son, I could see that the son was controlling both of them by using the divide-and-conquer tactic well known to all children. Keep the parents fighting and use them to get what I want.

The fact that this self-serving tactic was destroying his parents' marriage was of no interest to the son. The parents believed that they were doing the right thing by supporting their son. They failed to see the real cause of their marital distress: their failure to nurture and prioritize the marital dyad and be responsible, effective parents. They had created an extremely self-centered child who felt entitled to everything he desired, without any sense of personal responsibility or consideration for anyone else.

After several sessions I was able to alter their thinking by employing a second order change strategy, concentrating on their role and responsibilities as parents. I suggested that although they thought they were doing right by letting their adult son remain at home, they were denying him the opportunity to be independent and take responsibility for himself. And since it was their responsibility to teach him to be independent and responsible, allowing him to remain at home was *unfair to him*. After a few more sessions, they agreed to ask him to move out on his own, for his own benefit. He of course did not like their decision, but they stuck together and he moved out. Their marriage immediately improved.

Pathological Characteristics of the Adult Child

Reaching the age of chronological adulthood does not ensure that an individual is an adult psychologically. Psychologically immature adults, those who are over sixteen but think and act like children, have characteristics that are inappropriate, destructive, and indicative of immaturity and poor mental health.

Adult child characteristics include:

- *Self-centeredness:* everything is about me and what I want.

- *Dependence:* financially and/or emotionally reliant on someone other than themselves.

- *Irresponsibility:* refusal to accept blame when wrong or initiate responsible actions on their own.

- *Avoidance:* Having to be told to do things and resisting efforts to make them occur. Absence of a work ethic. Living for today with no thought or plans for the future.

- *Self-defeating and self-destructive behavior:* constantly failing or harming self by being irresponsible.

- *Chronic forgetfulness:* the goal is to avoid taking responsibility.

- *Aggressive or passive aggressive behavior:* using intimidation, helplessness, guilt, and revenge to manipulate and control others.

- *Learned incompetence:* continual failure to learn and do things on their own. However, this is accompanied by the ability to do the things they want to do.

- *Living in fantasy:* isolating and pretending instead of doing.

- *Relationship deficits:* inability to foster and maintain healthy adult relationships.

The Immature Pathological Mind: Divided and Destructive Thinking

Feeling good about who one is and being able to find fulfillment and experience a life of psychological quality is dependent on the individual's ability to have faith in the workings of his mind (self-efficacy). When a person has trust in his mind, he knows what is real and what is false. He trusts in his ability to know what is beneficial for him. He knows what is harmful. He has faith in his ability to learn anything he needs to know to make his life better. His mind is his best ally. It provides him with truth and direction. Because his mind knows constructive beneficial truth, it both guides him and holds him accountable for staying the course. His mind is his advocate. It is not his enemy.

An individual with a divided, troubled self has learned to avoid, deny, and distort truth. He therefore does not and cannot make sound beneficial choices. He is not guided by truth, reality, or reasoned thinking. For an individual with a troubled self, truth (reality) changes with the moment-to-moment experience of primitive emotions and with perceived immediate needs of the primitive-self. There are at best only hints of a meta-self. It is essentially powerless if it exists, because of the dominance of a dysfunctional primitive-self.

Reality to a troubled primitive-self is also living in a constant state of fear and cognitive confusion. At an early age, to survive psychologically, the individual with a troubled primitive-self choses isolation from the outside world and from the truth about himself. It is a child's only solution to the experience of confusion and bad feelings about himself. Developmentally, the cost of hiding from truth, the reality of oneself, is the failure to grow in a psychologically healthful manner and achieve psychological health and maturity. The afflicted individual will continue to develop physically and may grow a significant amount intellectually, but psychological development will be significantly limited or absent. The meta-self will be limited in development and will be dominated by the primitive-self. Eventually, the ultimate cost of being psychologically impaired early in life is a future filled with disappointment, failure, and for many, psychological self-destruction.

A mind that distorts or denies truth cannot build self-efficacy, faith in one's mind to know truth. Because an individual with a troubled self subconsciously avoids or distorts truth, he is unable to identify what is true even when he consciously wants to. He cannot judge what is true about his self or others. As a result, his troubled primitive-self lives in a fearful state of cognitive and emotional dissonance and confusion—at odds with and cut off from his real self. Because life requires us to make judgments, regardless of the quality of our thinking, the troubled person makes judgments that are self-serving, self-limiting, irrational, and harmful to himself and others. His reality is that he cannot trust his mind to know truth but has no idea why.

A person with a troubled divided mind must seek relief and resolution from constant and pervasive confusion and failure. He may look for something outside of himself to believe in that will provide him structure and emotional support, an externalized self-support object. He may choose to live in isolation from others, either physical or emotional, to be safe from harm. Or he may seek constant confirmation and reassurance about his self by being dependent on other people to make decisions for him. He will become "other focused," where his perceived value as a person is dependent on constant approval from others. His attempts to feel good about himself will all be in vain. Outward attempts will fail because an individual governed by a divided and troubled mind does not trust his mind to know in whom or what he should place his trust. Therefore, internally, he experiences a vicious cycle of attempting to get confirmation by trusting others and failing.

Outside attempts to reassure or comfort the individual fall on deaf ears because he cannot trust his mind to know who to believe, especially when inside he knows the truth about himself. Even positive and valid feedback is rejected internally because the individual knows his real self and knows he does not let that real self be seen. He believes that his real self would be rejected. After all, he dislikes his real self, so how could anyone else value it? Life is experienced as one failure after another to find acceptance, understanding, reassurance, and fulfillment for a troubled self. As the years pass, ever-increasing psychic confusion, suffering, and failure become the dominant state of the person's internal existence. Escape from one's self through addiction and/or isolation from others provides temporary relief that eventually becomes destructive solutions that only exacerbate dysfunctional behavior.

In a person with a mind dominated by a primitive-self, the meta-self has remained in an underdeveloped state. The mind's major function of finding and applying functional truth never develops. Instead, the meta-self exists as an inactive powerless element in a mind dominated by irrational and destructive primitive beliefs.

Changing one's life for the better requires the awakening and development of the power and abilities that can only be established within one's meta-self.

Developing a meta-self begins with the conscious choice and commitment to identify, value, and actually live functional, beneficial truth. Seeking and living constructive truth requires the individual to become conscious of and challenge the validity of everything he has previously learned about himself and the world—without exception. Everything he has learned must be reevaluated to determine if it is valid, rational, and constructive truth. If what he believes to be truth is not rational, valid, and beneficial, it must be discarded in favor of something better. Then, as he discovers constructive truth, he must hold himself accountable for living it in all areas of his life. The value of learning and living constructive beneficial truth must become his most important principle in life.

As the reader, you may be wondering why knowing and living truth is so critical. If you are, this may be your primitive-self resisting. Ask yourself how long you could function or even survive without knowing what is true (real) and what is false. For example, how could you change a belief in your mind that is harmful and destructive if you do not know what that belief is? It is impossible to evaluate and change a faulty belief if you are unaware of its existence. Knowing the truth about your current beliefs, especially about you, is the only way to effect real and qualitative change for the better in your life. Additionally, your ability to determine truth about your own inner experience and belief structure determines the level of your ability to discern truth externally, in other people and in the world in general.

Characteristics of a Psychological Adult

- thinking and feeling good about who one is as a person—and being accurate

- being physically, intellectually, and psychologically responsible (externally and internally)

- being conscious of and responsive to objective reality

- having reasoned thinking as the default thinking system; forming and living rational principles and values

- having internal confidence about one's self to achieve chosen goals

- being cognitively and behaviorally competent

- demonstrating genuine caring and empathy for all

- being competent interpersonally—the ability to get your emotional needs met in relationships

- being able to nourish one's self through being productive and achieving

- pursuing physical, intellectual, and psychological self-development as a lifestyle

These characteristics are corollary principles of the three foundational meta-principles: living in reality, reasoned thinking, and lifelong psychological growth. The meta-principles will be explored in greater detail in chapters 7–9.

The Challenge of Psychological Growth

To become someone they are not, the individual must have the courage to challenge what he has been taught to believe about everything. This is particularly true about the core beliefs he was taught at an early age to believe about himself. He must open up to repressed information about himself. He will need courage to challenge his primitive-self's resistance to his conscious awareness of his real self. Then he will be ready to open his mind to new ideas and be willing to risk moving in the unknown direction they may require. He must decide to evaluate all beliefs for validity and elect to live only those beliefs that can be substantiated through experience and reasoning as functional truth. Courage is the primary motivator of the meta-self, the adult healthy self. Challenging himself to reveal his core beliefs to his conscious awareness is accomplished by, and indicative of, his meta-self being engaged and taking constructive action.

The natural development of mental health can be observed in the person's ability to change, to maintain a functional mental balance between his current psychological organization of reality and his openness and ability to integrate new forms of experience, which may or may not change his current perception of reality. Being mentally healthy requires possessing the ability to assimilate a wide range of experiences of self and others while still maintaining the integrity and stability of the present psychological self-structure. The ability to maintain an optimum balance between a current, stable sense of self and being open to new learning enables psychological growth.

For example, when couples decide to marry or simply cohabitate, psychological change is inevitable. Both partners will be challenged to adapt to this new life experience. If they have not lived with someone before, they must learn how to mesh as an adult couple in a close or intimate relationship. Sharing, compromising, problem solving, and emotional risk taking are examples of activities that challenge an individual's previous perception of self and require change.

A mentally healthy individual will be able to integrate constructive belief changes while still being able to maintain a psychological boundary or separateness of self. A less healthy person will have problems that, depending on their degree of severity, may or may not be easily identified, owned, or surmounted. For example, an individual may be unable to compromise toward the needs of his partner. Another individual may panic because of too much uncontrollable compromising due to an inability to maintain psychological boundaries between self and others, especially those relationships where caring for a person makes the person most vulnerable.

The same process of integrating change would be necessary if the couple decided to divorce. There is both a legal divorce and a psychological divorce to process and transcend. Psychologically, both the initiator of the breakup and the spouse that has been rejected must accept the death of the relationship as they knew it, heal the psychological wounds, and adjust to being alone. Finally, each party must reintegrate to the singles' world as either a single parent or single without children.

Through the exposure and assimilation of new experiences, including bad ones, a healthy self expands in complexity and moves toward the realization of psychological maturity and the fulfillment of individual potential. The inability to incorporate new experience leads to the blocking of natural self-development and all the maladies associated with impeded or limited self-growth. In the worse cases, emotional crises can trigger a psychological regression. For example, individuals going through a divorce often suffer a loss of self-esteem. Usually this is a temporary condition. However, in many instances the individual makes changes in beliefs that are negative and mentally unsound. A worsening of already low self-esteem, permanent fixation on anger, and chronic distrust of the opposite sex are typical examples.

7

Reality, Reasoning, and Responsibility: Cornerstones of Mental Health

Mental illness, at its most basic level, is a thinking problem.

When people meet for the first time, they ask each other questions that will help them form a general impression and determine their significance and acceptability. Questions asked often include "What do you do," "Are you married," "Do you have children," and "What are your political and religious affiliations?" The answers help people categorize each other in relation to themselves. People seek commonality, shared values. Their answers represent their beliefs about what is true and significant to them.

As human beings, we are responsible for our own welfare and the welfare of the world we live in. We are responsible for preserving and improving our world for our own benefit as well as for the benefit of those who will follow. We assume that responsibility by first recognizing what is real and what is not real. This is qualitatively different from creating reality that is false and based on our refusal to use reasoned thinking, deferring to the majority opinion, or distorting or denying what is real to avoid internal psychological distress.

Mental illness, at its most basic level, is a thinking problem. Denying reality is mental pathology's most common dysfunctional behavior. To believe or pretend something is real when it is not is to lie to one's self. Lying to one's self, especially about one's self, is a common symptom of mental illness. Accepting a lie as truth must be supported by creating more lies. This process will adversely affect thinking, causing contradiction, confusion, absurdity, and eventually an inability to know what is real.

Acceptance of reality, on the other hand, is the initial and primary principle of establishing, regaining, or maintaining mental health. Each person has a responsibility to decide what is real and what is not real. *Mental health begins with accepting actual reality.* It also begins by taking responsibility for being and doing what is rational, functional, and beneficial for oneself and for others. It is each individual's choice and responsibility to take constructive control of his mind by learning to identify and accept what is real and true. The only means by which an individual can identify what is real and true is through the use of reasoned thinking: meta-principle #2 (see chapter 8).

An Overview of Three Meta-Principles: Foundational Elements of Mental Health

The realization of mental health must begin with a philosophy about its elements that define the experience of psychological quality. As a philosophical foundation, I propose three meta-principles as values that form the psychological underpinning of mental health.[1] *All subsequent constructive beliefs, values, and competencies are created as congruent corollaries of these three principles.*

Eric Fromm described a mentally healthy person as an individual who lives productively, guided by the principles of having faith in himself, reasoned thinking, and love.[2] Having faith in one's self is having a positive self-concept. Next, an individual must master the cognitive skill of reasoned thinking as the only means to know truth, be it objective or functionally subjective. Finally, love of life

---

1   See C. Franklin Truan, *Meta-Values: Universal Principles for a Sane World* (Tucson, AZ: Fenestra Books, 2004).
2   Erich Fromm, *The Sane Society.*

and mankind is a motivating principle to do what is good for all, and especially for one's self.

Fromm's viewpoint was based on the assumption that, with any subject or problem, there are such things as right or wrong, satisfactory or unsatisfactory. Fromm applied these principles to the identification of solutions to the problems that arise in confronting existence as a human being.[3] His principles are the means to determine what is real and true in order to provide man with an effective means to understand and meet the challenges that life presents.

The following three meta-principles are presented as the foundational building blocks of true mental health. These meta-principles are imperatives in the establishment or preservation of mental health.

Meta-Principle #1: To Know, Value, and Live Functional Reality (Subjective Truth)

To value reality is to pursue and accept what is real (true) about one's self and the external world and to reject what is not true. What is real or true is so because it is supported by objective facts and reasoned thinking. Living in reality requires the pursuit of objective accuracy in the individual's perception of himself (internal reality)— the truth about who he really is. An individual's ability to accept who he is allows him to see who he wants to become. Additionally, both internally and externally, living in reality requires living *consciously* in the present instead of dwelling in the past or fantasizing about the future. *The experience of psychological quality in life exists only in the present.*

Meta-Principle #2: To Acquire and Consistently Practice Reasoned Thinking

Thinking with reasoning is the pursuit and prioritization of logical, unbiased knowledge and understanding. Because understanding without action does not exist, the individual must act on this understanding—to live the functional truth gained through reasoning. *Reasoning guides the thinking and actions of the mentally healthy.*

---

3   Erich Fromm, *The Sane Society*, (New York: Fawcett Publications, 1955).

Because mental illness is a thinking problem, psychological well-being is dependent on *how well* we think, including the functional validity of our methods of thinking and the qualitative substance of our conclusions. Reasoning, a thinking method, requires the volitional, objective, and active pursuit of knowledge and understanding by focusing on the identification of truth that is compatible with reality—the essence of things and processes.

In the psychological realm, reasoning includes the productive integration of thinking and feeling, logical congruent concept formation, and self-evaluation. Reasoned thinking is directed toward the areas of problem solving, selecting constructive goals, and choosing beneficial beliefs, values, and virtues. Reasoned thinking is also the only method for determining ethical/moral principles for healthful psychological living with ourselves and others. *Reasoned thinking is man's only functional method for identifying truth, be it objective or subjective in nature.*

Meta-Principle #3: To Foster and Maintain a Lifestyle of Personal Psychological Growth

Psychological growth toward maturity is both a fundamental value and a way of life. Growing or developing psychologically requires adopting a lifestyle that prioritizes learning as a constant lifelong process in all domains of human life—physical, intellectual, and psychological. The need for the prioritization of growth is especially necessary in the most important domain—the psychological domain. Psychological learning includes increased knowledge in self-awareness, self-understanding, self-advocacy, and self-evaluation. It also includes the pursuit of growth of interpersonal knowledge, understanding, and competence (see chapter 9).

Together, the meta-principles are the foundational building blocks of true mental health. They are the essential and primary psychological and interpersonal principles for all people, regardless of culture, race, gender, or any other social variable.

Successful assimilation and application of these meta-principles is evident in the individual's interactions with himself and his environment.

Specifically, the individual demonstrates in his beliefs and actions in the:

- ability to trust in one's mental capacities to see truth, solve problems, select goals, and develop programs to achieve them;

- sense of personal faith in one's self;

- belief in one's value as a person being equal to all others;

- belief in one's adequacy to achieve in love, work, and play;

- ability to love and to believe one's self to be lovable;

- ability to treat one's self and all others with respect, tolerance, and kindness that is balanced by respect for truth and accountability;

- ability to be interpersonally competent and to find fulfillment in interpersonal relationships;

- objective capacity for one to accept and adapt to new knowledge—open-mindedness; and

- psychological independence—living in a state of psychological autonomy where the individual is independent from faulty, destructive beliefs that permeate society.

The three meta-principles are mental health–promoting values that are interdependent in that successful ownership and application of each requires the amalgamation of all three.

Introduction to Reality/Truth

First and most important in attaining or maintaining mental health is the quality of the relationship the individual develops with himself. Does he genuinely like and value who he is? Is he his own self-advocate? Is he in good company when he is alone? Can he rely on his mind to know truth? Does he have faith in himself?

Is he competent interpersonally? Does he have and project self-confidence?

With regard to the self, living in reality/truth begins with the objective pursuit of accurate self-knowledge, self-understanding, and self-acceptance. Achieving these are also the first step toward constructive self-evaluation and real psychological growth. Knowing one's real self is not only about knowing one's positive traits but also knowing one's deficits. Remember, being aware of one's deficits and negative self beliefs is the necessary first step in correcting them.

What Is Truth? Is There Such a Thing?

To live truth is to know and live what is right, fair, relevant, just, considerate, and psychologically beneficial. It requires the ability to determine functional *subjective* truth through reasoned thinking. To live truth, an individual must hold himself accountable for cognitive validity, congruence (no contradictions in beliefs), consistency, and functionality of thoughts and feelings. By making life a continuous conscious process of identifying and living the best functional truth, a person will be able to construct a set of principles that will provide productive direction in his journey of psychological growth and fulfillment as a human being.

As stated previously, the first principle of mental health is the consistent ability to discern subjective truth. However, the meaning of truth varies greatly among people. In general, *most people believe that real truth about anything is what they already believe*. They accept as true their beliefs, feelings, or opinions just because they have them. Regard for their origin or validity is absent; instead, they maintain that everyone else is wrong if they do not hold the same belief.

Another major group believes that there are many truths about anything and that each person may decide what is true. These people believe that everyone should respect their proclaimed truth and not challenge its veracity. This faulty belief is the premise and major concept supporting the currently popular term "diversity."

Accepting all beliefs as truth is also a major belief among religions—at least publicly. First, each faith has its own beliefs or doctrines. They are aware that other religions hold many different beliefs as reality. Whose beliefs are true? The solution to this dilemma is irrational but effective to believers taught not to reason. The unspoken rule among religions is, "I will not publicly challenge your particular set of beliefs (myths) if you do not challenge mine." They agree to disagree and to be silent about the disagreement. The irrationality or absurdity of anyone's religious beliefs is not addressed. Each religious group keeps their version of truth safe from scrutiny.

The destruction of the World Trade Center was a gruesome example of irrational fundamental religious beliefs justifying a horrific act. Instead of placing blame on the irrational and destructive nature of religious beliefs held as truth, the cause of the destruction and murders of thousands of people were placed on the vague construct of "terrorists." The perpetrators were of course radical extremists, but the underlying reality is that irrational religious "truth" justified their horrendous actions. Only a few blamed or even challenged their irrational religious beliefs. A historical look back at the Christian Crusades is also relevant in that it points out the same subjective irrational perception justifying the Crusades. Only a minority of historians maintain that Christians were wrong to force their religion on anyone and murder anyone who refused. Christian authorities and believers avoid the subject.

To my way of thinking, truth is important; in fact, it is vital. It holds people accountable for their actions. If an individual can accept lies as truth in one area of his life, he is likely to accept them in all areas. If an individual lies to himself, he will not be able to trust his mind to tell him what is real or true in any given situation. His lying is going to cause not only problems within himself but is also going to create problems in his relationships.

At one time during undergraduate school, I was a political science major. My professional aspirations included becoming a congressman. In one of my first classes, my professor was a former United States congressman during the Kennedy administration. After getting to know me and my goals, he advised me to consider the fact that in order to become a congressman and remain one, it would be necessary for me to give up my integrity. I would have to learn to lie for a living. I changed my major to philosophy. Knowing and living truth is critical in developing faith in one's real self. It is also the basis of integrity, a characteristic of mentally healthy people.

Meta-Principle #1: To Know, Value, and Live Functional Reality (Subjective Truth)

Living in reality requires the constant pursuit and acceptance of what is real and the rejection of all that is not real. Mental illness, be it subclinical, neurotic, or psychotic in degree, is the consequence of a mind that is not able to fulfill its functions. Beneath these abnormalities is always the mind's alienation from reality and truth. Developing and maintaining mental health begins with accepting reality, especially the individual's actual perception of himself.

The fact that a majority of people believe something to be true is not a sound basis for accepting it as so.

Awareness and Acceptance of Reality

During childhood and adolescence, each individual develops the cognitive processes and learns beliefs that will shape his thinking and behavior for a lifetime. Once formed, these beliefs and processes are the perceptual window through which truth is formed. Truth in this context includes tasks such as determining what is real and relevant, forming decision-making processes to determine actions, and developing core beliefs about one's self. Some of this cognitive learning process is directed and/or limited by genetics, but much, if not most, of the thought processes and all of the belief content is learned through interaction with the environment. Once learned, these mental processes and beliefs become *ingrained mental habits,* dictate how thinking happens, and determine what content is included or excluded. The quality of the individual's conclusions as to what is reality and truth is determined by the quality and breadth of content available and the quality of his learned mental thinking processes.

Mental health is determined by how well one's mind works and the functional quality of what has been learned. To represent mental health, thinking processes and conclusions must conform to reality. Individuals who are poor reasoners and those who are not mentally healthy are to varying degrees closeminded and ruled by the learned avoidance of reality. Mentally healthy people have a mostly unobstructed capacity for reality-bound cognitive functioning coupled with an openness to all relevant content. This capacity is called cognitive objectivity. At its best it combines both cognitive and emotional content.

If the individual's thought processes, feelings, and beliefs are in conflict with reality, or in conflict with each other, they will be harmful to the person and to others. This harmful pattern gradually leads to psychological and behavioral dysfunction and, depending on the degree of impairment, eventual self-destruction. Mental illness is the result of learned and prolonged denial or inability to see and live reality (truth).

Because living in reality and prioritizing truth are at the very core of being mentally healthy, an individual who was not lucky enough to be taught this principle as a child must make the conscious choice to do so as an adult. It is a choice to live constructively in reality and to reject all previous learning that is destructive to himself and others. Living truth requires knowing what one really believes about everything and being able to *substantiate its validity*. It also requires that those valid and beneficial beliefs be actually lived. Beliefs and values professed but not lived are not real.

Subjective and Objective Truth

Living mentally healthy requires identifying and accepting reality and seeking functional truth through reasoned thinking. Reasoned thinking is the pursuit of subjective truth that is logical, functional, ethical, and beneficial. Functional means that it works to provide effective and beneficial meaning and performance in the individual's life. Functional truth that is determined through reasoned thinking is not psychologically limiting, harmful, or destructive. It is beneficial to the individual's growth as a person and to his quest for value and fulfillment in life.

It's vital that the reader understands what I mean when I talk about the importance of knowing and living truth, and what the difference is between the different types of truth that affect our lives on a daily basis. Trusting one's mind to know truth must not be taken for granted. Let's begin the discussion about truth by exploring its nature and looking at typical processes people use to identify it.

Truth can be divided into two classes, objective truth and subjective truth. *Objective truths* are few in number and are absolutes. They are simply a priori knowledge and no alternative to their existence as truth is possible. They are self-evident. The most basic example of an absolute truth is man's very existence or the fact that we all will die. Objective truth comprises only a very small portion of what people live as truth.

The majority of truths we identify and live are *subjective truths* — man-made truth. Man-made truth is what a person or group of people decides to believe. It is subjectively conceived through man's thinking for better or worse. In the psychological realm of human existence, we are concerned with the *quality of subjectively conceived truth*. Subjective truth is good and acceptable only if it is logical and beneficial to man's well-being. In other words, does it work, and is it good for man's mental health and growth as a human being? Additionally, is it good for others or at least not harmful? An obvious example of a beneficial subjective truth is universal agreement that it is wrong to murder. Yes, it is true that there are exceptions. That is the gray area of rational thinking where most truth resides. Here is where mental health and reasoned judgment are called into play to determine subjective truth on a case-by-case basis.

Another less contentious and necessary example of functional subjective truth is the beneficial practice of adopting and following traffic laws. Wearing seat belts in automobiles is another example. Without these laws the highways would be nothing but chaos, and many more lives would be lost annually.

It is also true that there have been many laws that were proven to be arbitrary or untenable. As an example, prohibition, an attempt to make people stop drinking alcohol, was a huge failure. People were determined to ingest alcohol even if it meant breaking the law. The use of other drugs excessively and illegally is another example of the failure of law to control human behavior. Tens of thousands of people are dying annually from drug overdoses. The government's war against drugs has been a massive failure.

The truth behind these examples is that personal responsibility cannot always be legislated or enforced. Perhaps we should look deeper for the true causes of irresponsible destructive behavior. I believe that in the case of alcohol and drugs, our search would lead again to mental illness centering on a negative sense of self. Irresponsible and destructive behavior can most often be traced to psychological ignorance or illness.

Whose Responsibility Is It to Identify Truth?

About this time, some readers may be saying to themselves, "Truth is a difficult if not an impossible thing to know. Who am I to presume to know truth? What makes this guy (the author) think he knows what truth is?" These are fair questions. The answer begins with the fact that every individual must decide what is true many times each day. In life we all must make judgments about what is true and what isn't. The real question should be, "How well do I make judgments and identify truth?"

If an individual is to be mentally healthy and experience psychological quality, his thinking and actions must be justified by the standard that his subjective truths constructively enhance his existence without impeding his mental health and psychological development.

My goal is to present a discussion both as to the nature of truth and the methods man uses, for better or worse, to determine it. As the reader, your responsibility is to decide if I make sense or not. One of my important principles for living involves deciding truth when someone disagrees with me. My principle states that in order for me to change my mind to another person's way of thinking, he must make better sense to me than I have made to myself. My role is then to be open-minded about the potential validity of his view. This means that I will really listen to his view and give it consideration in part, and as a whole. For example, as someone reads this book, it is their responsibility to decide what truth is. If what I am presenting does not make sense, reject it and keep looking. Just be sure you are open-minded to ideas that challenge what you believe to be true.

As stated, determining truth is something we all attempt to do every day of our lives. However, our efforts can be for better or worse depending on the quality of our thinking. The saying "garbage in, garbage out" applies. Poor thinking produces poor conclusions. Faulty (irrational) thinking results in faulty conclusions. Thinking negatively about one's self, coupled with the lack of reasoning, will invariably lead to erroneous, irrational, and destructive conclusions about what is true about one's self and the world.

Hopefully, common sense tells us that all that is believed to be true by us and everyone else is not. This error in belief is easier to observe in another person's behavior than for one's self. If a person is objectively self-aware, then he has observed that his own experience is full of examples where he was certain something was true and later found out he was mistaken. In fact, we are all wrong about something almost daily. We as humans have a propensity to discount or ignore this fact about ourselves.

People who are mentally sound pay attention to their thinking and behavioral mistakes and learn from them. Perceptions and decisions based on erroneous beliefs are discovered and replaced with new rationally identified facts and beliefs. People who are less than healthy do not evaluate their thinking or do so with more faulty or biased thinking. They lack objectivity and insight about themselves and therefore repeat the same faulty thinking again and again. Everyone does not learn from experience.

It should also be obvious that people generally disagree about almost everything. Can they all be right? In other cases, millions of people may erroneously believe something is true. If many people believe that something is true, does that always mean it must be true? If something is true in one situation or time is it always true? People used to believe that the world was flat. People also believed that the moon was a god, or was made of cheese, or that man could never travel to its surface. Historically men and women have been burned at the stake because others believed them to be wizards or witches. Man's history is filled with examples of mistaken beliefs. The fact that a majority of people believe something to be true is not a sound basis for accepting it as so.

To be mentally healthy, an individual must have an effective method for determining truth and a standard for assessing the validity of his thinking. *As humans, our only means of determining truth is through reasoning.* Subjectively perceived truth must hold up to cognitive evaluation as being rational, verifiable, and beneficial. Truth that is valid and beneficial is found solely through reasoned thinking—not by following subjective emotions or simply desiring something to be true. On an individual level, and contrary to popular opinion, *the act of simply believing something is not sufficient grounds for its validity.*

Every individual should observe how he currently decides what is right or wrong or what is true or false. He should know how his mind determines truth and what his mind's method or system is. Most people are unaware of their minds' processes, if they even care. They just assume they know what is true. Many more wait for others to tell them what is true or what to believe.

Everyone makes decisions regarding truth numerous times every day of their lives. What time should I get up? What should I eat for lunch? Was Tom lying to me? How much of this medicine should I take? Why do I put off exercising when I know I should? Who is the best person to vote for? Why did my husband leave me? What will happen to me after I die?

These are all questions that require a person to decide what is true. And, in every case, the truth chosen will be for better or worse in that it is either accurate or inaccurate, rational or irrational, and beneficial or harmful to one's self or others. It is every individual's responsibility to make constructive and beneficial choices. Remember also that all choices lead to consequences, and they too are the responsibility of the individual making the decisions.

Next are typical examples of attitudes and behaviors about identifying truth.

Typical thinking deficits observed in nonreasoning individuals:

- They simply want to believe it, so they do.

- They are used to being told what to believe by authority figures.

- They perceive it to agree with something they already believe.

- They "feel" that it is true.

- They hear it in a biased way to make it true.

- They refuse to hear what they do not want to believe.

- They are unable to separate what is relevant from what is irrelevant.

- They are unwilling to explore an idea thoroughly and tend to oversimplify.

- They are unwilling or unable to reason—and yet insist they reason well.

- They live in a perpetual state of fear of change.

- They refuse to learn (usually a defensive reaction to bias, the acceptance of ignorance, or a belief that learning is too much work).

How are the readers of this book going to decide, among all the truths I present, which ones are valid? Are they conscious of the mental processes they employ to decide truth? Will they have faith in their mind's ability to discern truth? In the next chapter and beyond, readers will have an opportunity to evaluate the quality of their thinking processes and the validity of their conclusions. I hope they will hold themselves accountable for being open-minded to new facts and beliefs and the potential for discovering new truth.

8

Reasoning and Logical Thinking

Rationality, the recognition and acceptance of reason as one's only source of [true] knowledge.[1]

—Ayn Rand, philosopher

META-PRINCIPLE #2: To Acquire and Consistently Practice Reasoned Thinking: The Pursuit and Prioritization of Logical Unbiased Knowledge and Understanding

Is your thinking rational, objective, open-minded? Is conscious reasoning a priority in your thinking process? Take this short quiz to assess your degree of reasoned thinking.

Answer "agree" or "disagree" to the following statements:

- I have my reasons for what I believe, and that's enough for me.

- Feelings are more important than the reasons for the feelings.

- God exists and no one should deny that.

- Individuals who kill someone should always be put to death.

- Some races of humans are better than others.

---

1   In Leonard Peikoff, *Objectivism: The Philosophy of Ayn Rand* (New York: Penguin, 1993), 221.

- I am often just right about something and nothing can change my mind.

- I should listen to people who are wiser than me to make decisions. Making decisions on my own could lead to trouble.

If you agreed with any one of these statements, you have both a problem being objective and, to some degree, a reasoning deficit. You are of course free to deny this contention, but what if it's true. Maybe you are being close-minded. Can you entertain the possibility that you could be wrong about yourself? Most people believe they are good at reasoning, but most are not. What you believe about anything could be wrong. Are you open to challenging your beliefs for validity? Are you open to learning to think with reasoning?

The following is a general definition of what it means to think with reasoning:

"Being reasonable means holding beliefs and views from which: 1) one can give true or probable evidence that, 2) actually (or sufficiently and relevantly) supports them. And it means, also, 3) having true or probable evidence about what is wrong with beliefs that oppose or challenge your conclusions or the truth or sufficiency of your evidence. For the only ways any views can be reasonably challenged are by the supported claim that, (1) the conclusion is not true, (2) the evidence is not true, or (3) the evidence is insufficient to justify the conclusion."[2]

Reasoning and Mental Health

Man's conscious self-awareness and his rational conceptual faculties are what make him unique in comparison to all living creatures. Man, alone, is aware of his existence and his inevitable demise. Man is gifted with the ability to think, and to think rationally, *but it is not a given that he will do so.* He must make the conscious choice

---

2   Rick Garlikov, "Reasoning," theoretical companion piece to "Making the Most of Your University Courses: What to Expect Academically at College," http://www.akat.com/college.html.

to learn to reason. He must decide to think with quality and hold himself accountable for the validity of his thinking. Reasoning is man's only effective method for determining what is real. He cannot know truth any other way. He can evade truth by deciding to deny reality, or he can make the volitional decision to develop his rational abilities. Even after learning how to think logically and rationally, quality thinking always takes a sustained conscious effort. It does not just happen automatically.

Man's mental health depends on which path he chooses. If he chooses to evade reality and attempts to create his own perception of what is real, he will suffer a significant psychological cost. Most principally, he will lose faith in himself. If he chooses wisely to maintain a purposeful focus on objective reality and align his thinking with truth, he will reap the positive consequences of this decision. He will experience a sense of constructive control over his life and develop trust in his mind and faith in himself.

Examples of Nonreasoned Irrational Thinking

> *It is reasonable to have your own opinion, but it's not reasonable or rational to choose your own facts.*

Thinking without reasoning takes many forms, but they all have one thing in common: their conclusions are based on irrational, emotion-based thinking, not objective, logical reality-based thinking. Following are a few of the most often used nonreasoned thinking forms:

The first form of faulty unreasoned thinking, and perhaps the most prevalent, is *dichotomous thinking*, better known as all-or-nothing thinking, or black-and-white thinking. It is the case where an individual sees events and the concepts in simplistic extremes. Once the all-or-nothing thinker has arbitrarily decided what is true, he only seeks and hears information that agrees with his arbitrary inflexible position. All other opinions and facts are rejected without consideration.[3]

---

3 P. C. Wason and P. N. Johnson-Laird, *Psychology of Reasoning* (London: B.T. Batsford, Ltd. 1972), 237.

The second form of faulty, unreasoned thinking is *overgeneraliza-tion.*[4] In this case the individual observes something that is perceived as true in one case, and immediately generalizes this observation to be true in all cases. This faulty thinking practice is known as the logical fallacy of *hasty generalization.*

The third type of faulty thinking is *faulty personalization.* In this case the individual imagines that negative events are caused by himself. This problem is particularly evident in individuals with low self-concept. Because they lack a strong independent sense of self, they attribute an inordinate amount of responsibility to their own actions. These individuals have a dependent need to please others and are therefore readily manipulated by others who see their weakness. Because they lack appropriate psychological boundaries and have not learned to trust their own thinking, they have no option but to blame themselves.

Dichotomous thinking, overgeneralization, and *faulty personalization* are just a few of many thinking behaviors that represent nonrea-soned thinking. These thinking deficits are not necessarily a sign of mental illness, but they are a sign of subclinical problems and deficits in interpersonal competency. A reasoning deficit will also contribute to a negative self-concept and limited intellectual and psychological development. The inability to reason may be partially genetic in origin, or the result of the absence of modeling by primary caregivers, and/or their inability to teach its tenets. I maintain that everyone is born with some range of ability to learn reasoning. Because reasoning is not taught as both a value and a necessary cognitive and interpersonal skill, many—if not most—people never become aware of their deficit or take the initiative to learn reasoning to their full potential.

Over time, the lack of reasoning ability, and irrational thinking, will result in a wide variety of psychological and interpersonal con-sequences. The most widespread result is the gradual deterioration of an already negative self-concept. Individuals who are lacking suf-ficient reasoning ability and have a negative self-concept are most

---

4   Robert J. Gula, *A Handbook of Logical Fallacies* (Edinburg, VA: Axios Press, 2002).

likely to become physically, intellectually, and psychologically dependent on others.

As life progresses these individuals do not grow psychologically, and they also experience continual diminishment of mental health. They learn through repeated confrontations with reality not to trust the content or conclusions of their thinking or the mental processes they use to arrive at truth. Although they may deny their diminishing belief in themselves to themselves and others, the result is a lifetime of ever-increasing psychological distress and interpersonal incompetence and disillusionment. Eventually all faith in one's self is lost.

What makes people so susceptible to believing things that are not true? I believe that the cause is largely due to how man has developed psychologically over thousands of years. First of all, we as humans are by necessity social animals—we live in groups. We learn to relate positively with others. We learn to accomplish things by using the strengths of the group and pooling efforts to survive and flourish. Therefore, we are to a large degree predisposed to agree and conform to the will of the majority. We conform and compromise, go along with the majority for the sake of the community and to be accepted. We are taught, mistakenly, that acceptance and approval by others is the way to being liked and perhaps loved.

As an example, a major underlying purpose of our school system is to teach and require conformity in thought and behavior. Public schools were founded in nineteenth-century America with that goal in mind. Education authorities decide what is important for our children to learn, how they should learn to behave, and punish those who refuse to conform. As children we are taught *what* to think and believe. We are not taught *how* to think for ourselves. Learning to think for one's self is a choice made by a minority who have the insight and courage to challenge the norm.

The Internet: Meeting Place for the Irrational and Biased Person

Our great technological advances, particularly the internet, in recent history have further exacerbated the nonreasoning man's deficit of believing what others think instead of learning both how to think for himself and how to think rationally without an absurd amount of personal bias.

The nonreasoning thinker is a dependent thinker. He must seek out others to relate with that believe, think, and feel the same way. It's much easier for an individual to believe he has the truth if many people agree with him. He probably does not know that the number of people who believe something has nothing to do with its validity. To make matters worse, likeminded people can always be found, regardless of what you believe. The internet attracts all kinds of people because it is a place of free expression without any controls for rationality or veracity. It is quite evident that virtual relationships on the internet are replacing real life relationships, such as religious gatherings, as the major place to share erroneous irrational beliefs and get them confirmed as truth. Groups of like-minded believers become increasingly more convinced by their own selective and/or distorted facts that they hold the truth. Anyone who disagrees is considered stupid or dangerous, and perhaps also an enemy.

Our increasing preference for selective facts, or alternative facts according to politicians, that fit our personal biases, is fast becoming the new accepted custom. Unlimited access to any information, any facts, any beliefs on the World Wide Web, is causing as much psychological harm as it has contributed good by being an unlimited source of fallacious intellectual information. False information presented as facts, be it from the internet or any other source, that is heard over and over again becomes fact in the minds of ignorant, biased, and nonreasoning people.

Unfortunately, simplistic, biased, and irrational conclusions based on erroneous facts is the human norm with or without the internet. It has always been with us. People believe what they want to believe and ignore or attack anything that challenges those beliefs. Man's enduring ignorance in the psychological realm continues to impede man's growth toward mental health, maturity, and even peace among all people.

Man's refusal to learn from his own history, or even to see it and report it objectively, is a constant source of amazement to me. For example, it has taken man many thousands of generations to *begin* to believe in equality of all people. Man has forever condoned slavery until just recent times. Throughout the history of man, people of all cultures and religions have created subjective, irrational, destructive beliefs and laws to subjugate other human beings for their self-centered use and abuse. Power has always trumped reasoning and rationality.

Mankind and individual man continue to create erroneous self-serving belief structures to suit their immediate purposes without regard for their own psychological well-being and the rights and well-being of others. The solution for mankind's ever-increasing irrational thinking and irresponsible and destructive behavior is the same one it has always been. Man must recognize his ignorance, his self-serving destructive propensities. He must become aware of what he does not know and begin to take responsibility for valuing what is mentally healthful for all. Man must cease the blatant, self-serving refusal to accept and adhere to truth, own an underdeveloped reasoning ability, and educate himself and his progeny about how these deficits affect mental health.

Man must learn to value psychological development to the same degree we value intellectual development. Living objective and functional truth is an imperative to fostering and maintaining mental health. Reasoned thinking is man's only way to identify truth in any given situation. Man must learn to use his ability for reasoned thinking to improve the psychological quality of his existence and his mental health. He must also learn to reason for the sake of human survival. We now live on a figuratively small planet where reasoned thinking is a critical element in how the countries of the world will get along in the future. Man has yet to learn that what he chooses to live as principles and values has consequences.

Logical reasoned thinking is taught only as an elective in colleges, usually as a substitute for a math requirement. Reasoning is not required unless one is pursuing a major in philosophy. Why is reasoned thinking not a requirement in middle school? Why not in elementary school? The answer is simply and tragically that it is not prioritized as an intellectual value, let alone a psychological value.

The question must be asked, Why do we not value and teach our children *how* to think effectively for themselves? Could it be that once they learn to think rationally, they might then believe that they have the right to challenge everything they have been taught to believe as truth? They would hold us accountable for our irrational beliefs and for not living our professed values.

Integration of Rational Thinking and Feeling

The constructive integration of thinking and feeling are critical to experiencing psychological quality in life.

The experience of emotions is an intricate part of life, and they are fundamental to the experience of being human. They should neither be ignored nor overvalued as sources of truth. Like most of the things in life, feelings have productive and beneficial qualities while at the same time having the potential to be misleading, irrational, and even destructive.

Individuals with a negative self-concept use feeling in self-limiting and self-destructive ways. The primitive-self uses negative emotions to perpetuate its position of power within the mind. Negative emotions permeate a mind filled with negative self beliefs. Their purpose is to protect the primitive-self from being discovered because to be discovered is to lose power over the mind of the individual and be threatened with nonexistence. The primitive-self's strategy is to use negative emotions in two ways. The first is to lure the individual into a negative spiral of emotions about the self. The second method of control is to keep the individual convinced that shutting off from all emotion is the way to feel better about one's self. Both of these methods strengthen a negative self-concept and continuously lead the individual into harm's way.

Mental health requires that individuals be connected to their feelings at all times and that they have the ability to manage them constructively. In a healthy mind, feelings are information to be acknowledged and then evaluated for agreement with reality and validity. Most importantly they provide a doorway to an individual's thinking. Of particular importance is what an individual is thinking about himself. A mentally healthy individual is not only aware of his thinking and feeling but is also consciously and constantly assessing the validity of his thoughts. Individuals who repress their feelings do not have access to their true thoughts. Repression reinforces and gives strength to negative feelings and the thoughts that precede them.

Remember, mental illness is a thinking disorder. It is therefore the content and quality of what an individual is thinking that determines the presence and degree of mental health. A conscious connection to feeling and thought is critical in sustaining reasoned thinking and mental health.

Thinking as a Conceptual Process

Stated in cognitive behavioral terms, life is a cyclical process of *perceiving, thinking, feeling, and acting*. It is cyclical in that the process repeats itself continuously with or *without our awareness*. Taking constructive control of your psychological life is predicated on understanding this deceptively simple recurring process and making the conscious, volitional choice to learn how to productively manage its power over your life.

Perceiving+++++++++Thinking+++++++++Feeling++++++++++Acting

As children we are taught that thinking and feeling are different and competing systems that are usually at odds with one another. Depending on gender, we are generally taught to value either *facts we generate or facts given to us by others (boys) or experiences of emotions (girls)* as guiding principles in the process of conducting mental activity and behavior. In reality, to rely solely on one or the other is an ineffective and irrational unconscious habit, or else conscious strategy. Rational, productive, and beneficial thinking requires the balanced use of both thinking and feeling. The constructive integration of thinking and feeling are critical to experiencing psychological quality in life.

Rational conscious reasoning is a particular form of meta-thinking that incorporates emotional experience with focused logical thinking. Rational thinking that blends reasoning and emotion is learned through adopting the tenets of reasoning as a cognitive lifestyle and implementing its tenets and processes in all areas of one's life. Reasoned thinking cannot be applied selectively—as for example only in times of emotional crisis—and be expected to be effective. If one is ruled primarily by emotions or illogical thinking in times of noncrisis, it will not be possible to invoke the skills of reasoned thinking successfully during the experience of stress or emotional crisis. Reasoning must be a way of life.

Following is a general explanation of the processes involved in the constructive integration of thinking and feeling:

Perception: First, one perceives a stimulus—person, event, object, or thought. To perceive means to become aware of something's existence through one of the five senses—sight, hearing, touch, taste, or smell. A perception may or may not rise to the level of conscious awareness. Perception is a necessary condition for placing value but not solely sufficient.

Thinking/Cognition: Mental processing continues with a decision determining whether a perceived stimulus—person, event, object, or thought—is *significant*. This process may occur at either a conscious or subconscious level. If a stimulus has no significance to the individual, it means that no valuing occurs. If it is a conscious occurrence, a nonsignificant stimulus is ignored or discounted. The same is true at the subconscious level. If the stimulus is perceived as significant, then *value* is placed upon it.

Emotion/Feeling: Once significance and value are attached to a perceived stimulus, then feeling(s) based on the experience are associated with it. Attachment of a feeling response to the stimulus is not necessarily a conscious process. Thoughts and emotions can remain at a subconscious level, such as in the case of repression. The process of introspection (self-exploration) begins with getting in touch with feeling(s) and then tracing mental events to identify thoughts that proceeded.

Reasoning: Only when the individual becomes consciously

aware of his perceptions, thoughts, and feelings can reasoning be invoked successfully. Reasoning (focused logical thinking) includes:

- consciously acknowledging the experienced feeling(s) and associated thoughts;

- matching each feeling logically with the specific reason or reasons for the experience of that feeling ("I feel _____ because_____");

- combining feeling and reason to make meaning personal, concrete (clear and specific);

- assessing the personal meaning for validity, appropriateness, and rationality—what the origins of these thoughts, feelings, and conclusions are;

- determining the appropriate internal or external action and weighing the consequences of implementing it, keeping in mind that restructuring a plan for action may be necessary if potential consequences dictate a change in the chosen course of action is warranted; and

- overt/covert actions and evaluation—initiating action either externally in the form of behavior or internally in the form of self-discussion and additional exploration. Productive action always includes evaluation of thought processes and the appropriateness and effectiveness of all actions.

Thoughts and feelings comprise the basic content of the individual mind. At the mental process level, how well an individual thinks—the degree of his ability to use his mind effectively—determines the quality of his mind's content and therefore the validity of his conclusions.

A psychologically healthy person's cognitive and behavioral abilities involve the mental ability to:

- integrate feelings and thoughts into a constructive psychological product that allows the individual to better understand himself and his experiences and effectively communicate with others;

- solve the problems that life presents; and

- achieve goals through the identification and initiation of productive actions.

These abilities are dependent upon the results of reasoned thinking.

In Summary

The quality of an individual's self-concept is dependent on the development of his capacity for rational thought. Rationality depends on the commitment to the perception and adherence to reality and the development of reasoned thinking. Therefore, reasoning must be the dominant element and function of the mind to identify truth. All feelings have a cognitive origin, and that origin, or cause, is the thoughts that generate them. Feelings are important, but the reasons that cause the feelings and the validity of those reasons are more important.

The content of an individual's mind is a product of learning through experience. Reasoning is a skill of the mind that is either learned through constructive and beneficial early learning, particularly primary modeling and shaping, or it is a skill that can be consciously learned by an adult. Once rational thinking is mastered, it is an individual's primary source of self-confidence and self-efficacy. Reasoned thinking is the prerequisite for having reality-based good judgment, decision-making skills, and most important, faith in your mind to know truth.

9

Psychological Growth and Maturity

META-PRINCIPLE #3: *Psychological Self-Development*

Valuing psychological self-development entails fostering and maintaining a lifestyle of responsible psychological growth. In other words, psychological growth is the means to realizing psychological quality, and it is predicated on living the first two meta-principles as lived values.

The Psychology of Healthful Growth

Man's choices do not include whether he will change over the span of his lifetime but only whether he will change in a productive, healthful direction in response to the inevitable challenges that life presents.

Personal psychological growth is the productive and beneficial transformation of beliefs, attitudes, and behaviors in response to change, be it of the individual's own volition or imposed by outside forces. In informal terms, it is the birth of something beneficial in us—the transformation or evolution of one's self into something new and better. Personal growth is developmental change in a positive, healthful direction. For psychological man, that positive direction may be toward improved mental health, psychological independence, maturity, or increased interpersonal competence.

In the psychological domain, man learns through experiencing and from objectively evaluating and understanding those experiences. Constructive learning is only possible through rational, focused thinking that centers on the integration of reality-based facts and subjective experience. Whether an individual orchestrates change as a part of a productive lifestyle or has it thrust upon him as an inevitable part of life, it is a continuous part of human experience. Man's choices do not include whether he *will* change but only whether he will change in a productive direction in response to the inevitable challenges that life presents. Responsible self-development as a lived value means bringing constructive volitional focus and direction to the process of inevitable change. The individual must decide if he will allow the outside world and its authorities to direct the course of his life, or if he will use his own mind to examine and direct his response to change that is presented.

If we are mentally sound beings, we have a natural inclination and, if lucky, the learned desire to develop in all three domains of human functioning: physical, intellectual, and psychological. Psychological growth requires conscious self-awareness, self-examination, introspective understanding, and constructive action toward specified goals. Specifically, psychological growth is achieved through: the positive maturing and broadening of self-concept, the motivation and action toward achieving the realization of potential capacities and talents, and a lifestyle of increasing intrapersonal and interpersonal competency and contributing empathically and behaviorally to the welfare of ourselves and our relationships with others.

As presented in an earlier chapter, during early childhood, the responsibility for our psychological development is, for better or worse, in the hands of our primary caregivers; for example, being encouraged to explore and learn and being emotionally rewarded through encouraging responses for any attempts. A young child whose efforts to learn are appropriately responded to develops the desire to learn and also feels good about who he is. He will become increasingly more self-confident. By the child's teens, his self-confidence about himself as a person will enable the internal incorporation of motivation to continue his learning and psychological growth throughout his adult years. Outwardly, his confidence will be evident in his interpersonal competency and above-average sense of psychological independence.

Despite the fact that human beings have the ability to keep growing in all three domains of functioning throughout life—physically, intellectually, and psychologically—most people stop growing far short of their potential. In the intellectual domain, for example, the average person reaches their peak of intellectual attainment by the age of fourteen or fifteen. Daily newspapers reflect this by the fact that most of them are written in language that can be understood by a fourteen-year-old.

As stated earlier, psychological growth typically does not continue much beyond the period of adolescence for most people. Unfortunately for most people, once they have reached chronological adulthood, and because of their immaturity, change is not usually volitionally self-directed. Change is instead directed by outside forces such as changes in status or the occurrence of crises. A smaller percentage of individuals learn through experience to value and embrace change as part of life. For these lucky people, personal growth is actively pursued as a lifestyle. They learn to welcome change as a natural part of living and growing. When crises occur, and they will, they are viewed as life challenges and as opportunities for personal growth.

Psychological Maturity

Psychological maturity is realized by the successful development of man's conceptual, rational consciousness. Psychological maturity is evidenced by one's conceptual ability to have

an actively sustained process of identifying ones' impressions in conceptual terms, of integrating every event and every observation into a conceptual context, of grasping relationships, differences, similarities in ones' perceptual material, and of abstracting them into new concepts, of drawing inferences, of making deductions, of reaching conclusions, of asking new questions and discovering new answers, and expanding ones' knowledge into an ever-growing sum. (Ayn Rand, *The Virtue of Selfishness*)[1]

Rand's description of mature mental functioning is compatible with my four- and five-level capabilities presented in chapter 10. To be real and psychologically fulfilling, the mind's conceptual ability must be developed and practiced in all areas of one's life, in particular the psychological/interpersonal realm. It cannot be limited to intellectual or technical pursuits in one's professional life. All subsequent aspects of psychological maturity are derivatives of developing one's psychological conceptual faculties.

They include:

- acceptance of responsibility for one's own life and actions;

- acceptance of responsibility for long-range planning and the delay of gratification;

- an ability to remain emotionally stable under conditions of pressure, disappointment, fear, or anguish; and

- the ability to believe oneself capable of learning anything that is needed or desired.

The number of years lived is not the determining factor in the acquisition of maturity. As presented above, maturity is a psychological concept, not a physical or intellectual one. What is the difference between growing more mature and just growing older? Here are some general applied characteristics of the psychologically mature adult:

- a strong and positive sense of who he is

- his own and best self-advocate

---

1   Ayn Rand, *The Virtue of Selfishness*, (New York: New American Library, 1964).

- confidence in his ability to do and to learn

- accepts responsibility when asked and takes responsibility when needed without prompting

- believes in his mind's ability to know truth

- reasoning is his default mode of thinking; emotions play a secondary role

- good at identifying and solving problems

- outlook on life is mostly positive, despite what goes on in the larger world and all that has challenged his positive attitude in his personal life

- even-tempered for the most part and avoids conflict unless it is absolutely necessary

- sees life as not being all about himself; has time and energy to give to others

- performs tasks completely and to the best of his ability

- sets and keeps personal goals

- patient and can delay self-gratification

- enjoys learning as a lifetime process

- has control of the course and quality of his life as much as possible

- able to adapt to change when necessary

Values: Reflections of Maturity and Self-Concept

Every action above the level of instinct is based on an underlying learned value.

Values defined:

- to value anything is to perceive it as significant

- to value is to believe in something

- to value is to take action

- to value is to live what one values

Understanding the nature of values must include an explanation about what values are not. Values do not emanate from nature as intrinsic to man and are not a gift from a divine entity. Values are abstract conceptual creations of man's mind. Essentially our values express what we think should be real or true. Our every action above the level of instinct is based upon an underlying learned value. They are created, professed, lived or not lived, and even discarded according to our subjective will. Values are a product of our subjective thinking, for better or worse, depending on the quality of our thinking.

The values we choose to live determine the course and quality of our lives. *We are all required to choose what we will value, but we are not required to choose wisely.* To experience psychological health and quality, man must choose to value and live that which is actually good for him. By good, I mean the chosen values must be beneficial in that they contribute in some constructive manner to the individual's survival, development, or psychological nourishment—be it physical, intellectual, or psychological. Psychologically, good or beneficial values are not only necessary for sustaining mental health but also provide for man's need and desire for self-development and self-enrichment and enable successful interaction with his environment.

In the life of man, all purposeful action aims at the achievement of a value. In other words, everyone has and lives by values, and all decisions and actions are based on them. In the broadest sense, values are anything and everything a person deems to be of personal significance.

The values held by an individual express:

- degree of agreement with objective and functional subjective reality;

- attitudes toward the self—level of self-awareness, self-concept, self-esteem, self-efficacy, and self-confidence; and

- attitudes about what is possible in life, work, achievement, lifestyle, relationships, pleasure, existence, and intimacy.

The act of valuing is the mental and emotional act of preferring one object, action, idea, or person over others. As man perceives something, he defines its existence and thereby initiates the process of deciding its value. If he believes the idea or object of his perception is truth and it holds personal significance, it is valued and becomes part of his perceived and preferred reality. Once chosen, values act as principles, man's guides to thought and behavior. The content of those lived values is a critical factor in determining the level of mental health and personal fulfillment possible. For example, are the chosen values beneficial to the individual's self-image? Are the chosen values ethical?

The process of valuing begins with perception and ends with action since every action above the level of instinct is based on an underlying learned value. *Once formed, values govern everything the individual thinks and does.* If the individual is aware of the values driving his actions, he can both live those values more fully and consciously exercise the option to change any of them if they are detrimental to his welfare or fail to remain fulfilling. If an individual is not consciously aware of his values, they still will determine everything he does, from thoughts to actions. For those who are unaware of the values that drive them, value changes, for better or worse, are chance occurrences, generally the product of crises rather than conscious volitional choice.

The search for constructive values as ethical and beneficial principles for living is a quest for what will support man's betterment of himself and his fellow man. Once these values are identified, the challenge is to live them in a world that is both largely indifferent to constructive values and, by default, lives primarily by harmful values that are self-serving, irrational, contradictory, and/or inconsistently applied. They are absent of psychologically constructive content and instead reflect the psychological immaturity and self-centered needs of the individual.

In Summary

The principles and values chosen, and actually lived, by an individual are reflections of his character. At the same time, principles and values that are professed but not actually lived, also reflect character. The quality of one's self-concept is dependent on the content of his professed values and whether or not he actually lives them. An individual who is not aware of his values is still held accountable by himself at the subconscious level. Subconsciously he cannot get away with lying to himself.

The individual's relationship to reality, the quality of the self-concept, and his capacity for abstract reasoning are the determining factors in his ability to understand and hold himself accountable. A mentally healthy individual is aware of principles and values he holds. The extent of awareness depends on both the level of abstract intelligence and the level of mental health of the individual.

Mental health, psychological fulfillment, and maturity in life can only be realized through the conscious sustained efforts of the individual. Necessary to this effort is a personal philosophy that includes a set of principles and values for living that are based on objective and functionally subjective reality developed through reasoning and continuously tested and revised based on increased knowledge and experience.

Values are corollaries of principles and character traits of the individual. The content of these elements and whether they are reality-bound, beneficial, and actually lived helps determine the presence or absence of mental health. Underpinning all of these elements is the capacity for applying reasoned thinking.

As life unfolds, an individual experiences changing perceptions and a corresponding change in values brought about by volitional psychological growth and inevitable life crises. Consequently, principles, beliefs, attitudes, and behaviors will be modified throughout life. If one's core principles and values are sound, change is welcomed as a natural part of life in that it provides the opportunity for personal growth and fulfillment. However, if one's principles are negative—meaning they are based on a negative sense of self or erroneous perceptions of reality—continued psychological growth is not possible.

10

Elements of *Intra*personal Character

A Continuum of Mental Health and Interpersonal Competency Elements

Chapters 10, 11, and 12 present a detailed description of the elements that encompass mental health and interpersonal competency. Each element is presented in five levels that describe a continuum of attained psychological and interpersonal functioning. Level 1 describes the lowest level of psychological functioning and Level 5 describes the highest level.

Chart #1: Elements of Intrapersonal Character—concerns the internal characteristics that form the basis of mental health and provide the foundation for the interpersonal conditions and competencies presented in Charts 2 and 3.

Chart #2: Intrapersonal and Interpersonal Process Conditions—presents the transactional process conditions that are evident in all human interactions.

Chart #3: Intrapersonal and Interpersonal Competencies—describes the cognitive and interpersonal skills that are possible based on functioning of Charts 1 and 2.

General Comments about Functioning Elements and Levels

Levels 1 and 2 in all three charts define primitive-self functioning. They characterize psychologically underdeveloped or impaired individuals who can be classified on the continuum as immature, irresponsible, dysfunctional, harmful to self and others, or mentally ill. The particular placement on the functioning continuum is determined by degree of impairment. It is difficult for individuals assessed as functioning at Levels 1 or 2 to improve their level of functioning.

Level 3 is the first level of healthy mental functioning. At this level, psychological learning and growth is more probable than it is at lower levels. To do so, individuals must be able to own their deficits and accept responsibility for personal growth. They may or may not be able to manage their own growth individually. The assistance of a mentor or counselor who can help them be objective about themselves and knows how to provide additive direction in their growth process may be necessary.

Levels 4 and 5 represent those individuals whose mental health and interpersonal competency are above average. For these individuals exhibiting higher levels of mental health and interpersonal functioning, the charts provide a means to identify their characteristics and skill sets. At these advance levels of mental health and competency, individuals are able to manage their learning and growth programs for achieving psychological growth.

Selfratings and objectivity: The inability to be objective about one's self in self-report exercises is reflected in a variety of ways. People have difficulty being objective about themselves, even when they are able to see others objectively. For example:

- An individual cannot see or understand beyond (higher than) the level at which he functions.

- Any individual will have a tendency to overrate his functioning.

- The more dysfunctional the individual is, the higher he will mistakenly rate himself.

In my experience, it is difficult to train or treat those who function at Level 2 and below in multiple elements. Additionally, the older an individual is, the more difficult the change process becomes. In both cases real change requires a high level of determination to change. In any case, success, regardless of age or initial level of functioning, depends on the individual's *desire and ability* to change. *Finally, the actual ratings of an individual in self-concept, reality base, and reasoning are the most significant predictors of mental health.*

Elements of Intrapersonal Character

The first and most important element with regards to mental health is self-concept. Individual functioning levels observed in the elements of self-concept, reality base, and reasoning ability are the most critical determinates of possible functioning levels in most of the remaining mental health elements, and in overall psychological and interpersonal functioning. Following is a description of the intrapersonal elements that represent an individual's level of mental health and interpersonal competency.

Element #1: Self-Concept

Definition: The "self" is a specific term referring to the structure of a person's experience of himself. The self-concept is the subjective content of the self and is comprised of what the individual believes as truth about himself, his actual thoughts and feelings about himself as a person, and his quality in relation to the outside world.

Level 1: Self-Concept (Primitive-Self)

At its lowest and most primitive and destructive mark, Level 1, a negative self-concept is damaging to the life of the individual and to all those who come in close contact with him. The Level 1 individual lives psychologically disconnected from his real self. This means

Elements of Personal Character
Levels of Psychological Self-Functioning & Experienced Emotional Quality*

Chart #1

Characteristics (Intrapersonal)	Level 1: Primitive	Level 2: Primitive	Level 3: Mixed	Level 4: Meta	Level 5: Meta
Self-Concept — Self-awareness and quality of self-esteem	Disconnected from self and others; no empathy; self-destructive; words and behavior contradict	Partial self-awareness; divided self-connection to self negative; feelings dominate; may own poor self-concept	Generally positive self-concept; negative self blind spots cause inconsistent feelings, thoughts, and behavior	Positive self-perception; high self-awareness and esteem; trusts own judgment; self-assured and confident; consistent real-self connection	Self-integration complete; objectivity of self and others, even under stress; thinking and feeling integrated; values constructive, clear, and lived
Reality Base — Agreement with objective functional reality of personal thoughts, feelings, and actions	Little or no real self-awareness; denies negative self; blames others; cut off from constructive reality	Partial awareness of own thoughts and feelings; reality changes with subjective self-centered emotions	Generally aware of reality; thoughts, feelings, and actions consistent over time unless emotionally stressed	Objective awareness of reality; incorporates abstract concepts; holds truth as value; few blind spots under stress	Lives value of rational objectivity; reason integrates and guides emotion; lives in functional reality; no blind spots
Reasoning — Ability to logically/objectively conceptualize, organize, and integrate thoughts, feelings, and behavior	Literal and fact oriented; little connection with reality or objective reasoning with self or others; reasoning self-gain focused with no integrity	No concept formulation; sees basic pattern only; generalizes illogically; all-or-nothing self-focused thinking evident	Understands basic concepts; tracts logically but cannot see whole picture; objectivity and logical thinking falters when under stress	Formulates objective, accurate, and logical concepts; reasoning sound and consistent—even when stressed	Integrates concepts—introspectively and for others; continuity and congruence of concepts; reasoning insightful and additive
Value Structure — Productiveness of value structure	No redeeming values; no integrity; destructive to self and others; focus on immediate gratification	Real values mostly unknown; known professed values are vague, situational, or focused on self-gain	Lives some beneficial values; respects most values of others; has value deficits and blind spots; resistant to needed change	Values clear, constructive, congruent, and lived consistently; values change with new learning	Lives high integrity and strong principles with clear, fulfilling values; objectively and rationally integrates, expresses, and justifies all principles and values

Chart #2

Characteristics (Intrapersonal)	Level 1: Primitive	Level 2: Primitive	Level 3: Mixed	Level 4: Meta	Level 5: Meta
Achievement Orientation to reaching individual potential for achievement	Motivation nonexistent; no personal goals; focus on immediate self-gratification	Focus on survival only; goals immediate or low and inconsistent; lacks consistent work ethic and underachieves	Motivation without direction; focus on present; self-accountability inconsistent; goal-setting vague; new achievement minimal	Motivated with direction; self-starter with programs for success; short- and long-term goals evident and record of success	High achievement; success in multiple areas of life; provides direction to others; achievement a lifelong value
Power Type of power; methods of influencing behavior of others	Coercive: uses aggression, powerlessness, or suffering to manipulate others	Manipulative: focus on self-gain; uses passive-aggression, suffering, or helplessness; motivated by fear	Position power: uses title or rules; displays some situational personal power when not threatened	Interpersonal power: self-assured; uses constructive people skills in many areas	Interpersonal/admiration power: constructive leader; respected by friends; displays power in all settings
Initiative Orientation to action and assertive ability	Assertion is primarily aggressive for self-gain; acts constructively only when forced	Procrastinator: proactive when self-gain is possible and risk is minimal; lacks assertive ability; fearful of failure	Acts when encouraged or if positive outcome is probable; assertive unless emotionally stressed or high risk perceived	Constructively proactive with little need for direction; assertive with compassion and respect for others; functions well under stress	Develops and implements programs to achieve goals—personal and professional; high achiever in many areas; provides direction to others

*Interpersonal conditions are communicated at both verbal and nonverbal levels whenever two or more people are in one another's presence. These conditions communicate the speaker's personal attitude toward others and his own character and are predictive indicators of interpersonal competency.

his awareness of his negative self-concept is absent. He accepts no responsibility for his behavior regardless of its destructiveness. He functions in self-destructive ways both internally and with others. His perception of reality changes to fit immediate needs. Psychologically he is isolated from himself but also from others; therefore, there is a profound absence of internal empathy and understanding about himself and an absence of empathic connection with others. He acts as though he cares not for his own welfare or anyone else's. He lives in the here and now, focused on short-term self-gain and immediate gratification, without concern for consequences or the rights or needs of others.

Level 2: Self-Concept (Primitive-Self)

The Level 2 individual also functions and is dominated by a primitive-self that is, at best, limiting the awareness and conscious acceptance of his negative self-concept. Level 2 at its worst will eventually be destructive to the individual if it is not addressed and changed. Some awareness of the real self may be present, but it is rationalized as normal. Also evident is a divided self that is constantly in a state of cognitive dissonance and confusion. This individual will most likely be psychologically immature. Psychological functioning is at the level of a child. An adult healthy self, the meta-self, is only partially developed. These deficits are usually masked by a surface-self that has learned how to feign the surface behaviors of an adult in public. In private, the immaturity and dysfunction become readily apparent, particularly in troubled and destructive relations with others.

Negative feelings about the self and others dominate thinking and contaminate internal thought processes and external behavior. If the individual owns his negative self-concept, he does little to understand his deficits or improve the quality of his psychological existence. Over time psychological and interpersonal deterioration is inevitable without therapeutic intervention.

Level 3: Self-Concept (Mixed Primitive and Meta-Self)

Level 3 is where mental health first becomes apparent. The Level 3 individual has a generally positive sense of self. However, also evident are psychological blind spots that hide negative self-beliefs and interpersonal deficits that are limiting or harmful to the individual. Inconsistent and contradictory thoughts and behaviors are indicators of these blind spots. Poor reasoning and contradictory shifts in perceived reality may be evident. The individual may function acceptably in most situations unless placed in stressful or emotionally charged situations. Regression to lower levels of thinking and behavior will then be observable. These are areas where growth is needed.

Level 4: Self-Concept (Meta-Self)

Level 4 is marked by a highly positive and accurate sense of self and strong faith in one's personal values and interpersonal abilities. Thinking and behaving is mentally sound (congruent and consistent), based on the dominance of a fully functioning meta-self. *A higher degree of psychological independence from outside opinion is evident.*

Self-concept is positive and consistent over time, even at times of stress or crisis. There is an objective awareness of self that can be critical of behavior when necessary but it is tempered by a solid positive sense of self. Self-efficacy (faith in one's mind to know truth) is well established. The individual is a consistently strong self-advocate. A self-assured attitude and objectivity increase psychic energy and the ability to contribute to others.

The Level 4 individual trusts his judgement about most things yet is aware of when he does not know. The pursuit of knowledge over a broad spectrum of topics is common. Multiple competencies based on a strong positive faith in self and a willingness to learn and work are evident. He is able to perceive problems, initiate needed change, and hold himself accountable for sustaining self-change efforts.

Level 5: Self-Concept (Meta-Self)

A Level 5 individual possesses a consistently high positive sense of self and a high degree of psychological self-integration. This individual is a successful member of society but is psychologically independent from its conforming demands and its detrimental elements. He has an abstract big-picture ability to see real issues and is able to provide direction in specifying problems and achieving goals. This ability is true for self, with other people, and for issues in society.

At this highest level, the individual demonstrates high levels of abstract conceptual ability, objectivity, emotional awareness, and reasoned, directed thought and behavior. There is a conscious awareness of the innermost thoughts and feelings and consistent self-objectivity and objectivity about others. A high degree of personal integrity, self-esteem, and self-efficacy provide a base for stable self-confidence.

The Level 5 individual also displays the highest level of interpersonal abilities in all areas of life. These abilities are employed with congruently high levels of empathy and respect, adherence to functional subjective truth, and the needs and rights of others. Finally, a Level 5 functioning individual encourages and teaches others to live a positive, reality-based, self-affirming, and productive lifestyle.

Element #2: Reality Base

Definition: The individual's awareness and agreement with functional reality in thoughts, feelings, and actions.

Level 1: Reality Base (Primitive-Self)

This individual has little or no accurate sense of his true self, or he has partial awareness but doesn't care about it. If known, a negative self is denied. Blame always rests with others. Perception of external reality changes to match immediate needs. This individual perceives the world and its events only in a way that matches his internal fluctuating perception of reality. He ignores or denies objective facts.

Level 2: Reality Base (Primitive-Self)

There is partial awareness of real thoughts and emotions about himself. Thinking is immature, irrational, incongruent, or logically faulty. Reality changes with fluctuating self-centered emotions and the urge to bolster a shaky sense of self. There is an inability or refusal to accept responsibility or blame.

Thinking is self-centered, contradictory, and emotion-laden. The effects of his own behavior on others are often misinterpreted or goes unnoticed. This is evidence of an absent or limited internal empathic understanding and ability to connect well with others.

Level 3: Reality Base (Mixed Primitive- and Meta-Self)

At this level the individual is generally aware of reality, and it is valid and consistent unless emotionally stressed. Thought, feeling, and behavior are generally congruent. Regression is evident when unresolved psychological issues are emotionally triggered. Thought processes are generally in line with objective reality unless a subjective blind spot is triggered. Once a blind spot is triggered, emotions dominate and interfere with rational thinking.

Level 4: Reality Base (Meta-Self)

The Level 4 individual has an above-average objective perception of reality. He views and evaluates his own thinking and behavior for agreement with functional reality. He employs reasoning to understand and assess abstract concepts with a focus on subjective truth and reality. He regards reasoned subjective truth and reality-based objectivity as critical values. His thoughts and behavior remain stable and in touch with reality when under stress or in a crisis situation. Blind spots are few, if any.

Level 5: Reality Base (Meta-Self)

At this highest level, the skills and abilities of Level 4 are enhanced by the following traits: The Level 5 person consistently lives the value of rational objectivity in all areas of life. Personal principles and values are clear, constructive, congruent, and consistently lived in all areas of life.

At this level, the individual is capable of reading the subjective perceptions of reality observed in others and identifying faulty thinking. His reality-based thinking ability is guided by conscious reality-based principles and a superior reasoning ability. He will test other people's perception and acceptance of objective reality and challenge himself and others to identify the subjective reality that best fits the immediate situation. He also possesses a big-picture perception of the world that is based on the acceptance of truth and reality.

Element #3: Reasoning

Definition: The individual's ability to logically and objectively conceptualize, organize, and integrate thought, feeling, and behavior.

Level 1: Reasoning (Primitive-Self)

Thinking is confined to a superficial and literal view of mostly physical reality. Reasoning is absent and thinking is ruled by emotions. The individual's thinking may be immature, illogical, and incongruent and is primarily focused on defensively protecting a fragile sense of self.

Level 2: Reasoning (Primitive-Self)

At this level, there is limited ability to form basic functional cognitive concepts. Thinking is black and white—all or nothing. Basic concepts may be understood, but generalization attempts are usually illogical. Thinking and behavior is emotionally driven and self-focused. Responsibility in the form of blame is projected on others. Continuous criticism of others, either covertly or overtly, is evident. This individual will listen only to others with whom agreement is perceived. All facts and people that are not in agreement with personal beliefs are blocked. Thinking is usually void of reasoning, yet that fact is vehemently denied.

Level 3: Reasoning (Mixed Primitive- and Meta-Self)

At Level 3 there is an understanding of basic concepts and logical tracking but an inability to formulate and understand higher level concepts. When placed under stress, objectivity and logical thinking falters. Some beliefs may be rational and logical, while some will be absent of reasoning due to learned bias or the inability to reason beyond a basic level. There is no awareness of when thinking is reasoning based and when it is not.

Level 4: Reasoning (Meta-Self)

At Level 4 there is an above-average ability to form objective abstract logical concepts. Reasoning is sound and consistent even while stressed. Also evident is the ability to be additive to the opinions, beliefs, and conclusions of other individuals. There is a consistent ability to find common ground among differing opinions and provide workable solutions to complex problems and issues. *These abilities may be confined to an area of specialization.* This individual is able to discriminate when others cannot be reasoned with. When needed and appropriate, he is able to change his behavior to induce the other person to listen.

Level 5: Reasoning (Meta-Self)

In addition to Level 4 abilities, a Level 5 individual is able to introspectively integrate independent facts into new concepts and communicate clearly with others in explaining them. Reasoning is consistently reality-based, objective, insightful, and additive to the understanding of others. Superior reasoning and responding abilities make him a respected leader in all arenas of his life. He is respected by all, even those who disagree.

Element #4: Value Structure

Definition: Awareness of and quality of values. Degree of actually lived values versus professed but unlived values.

Level 1: Value Structure (Primitive-Self)

For this individual, values are both self-destructive and largely harmful to others. The absence of integrity and disconnection from self prevents any conscious awareness, constructive values, or self-accountability for destructive behavior. Immediate self-gratification is the individual's main value.

Level 2: Value Structure (Primitive-Self)

At this dysfunctional level, values are vague or unknown. If any are constructive or beneficial, they are lived sporadically and in self-serving token form. Verbal expression of values is superficial and absent of conviction. Behavior is inconsistent and results in being distrusted by others.

Level 3: Value Structure (Mixed Primitive- and Meta-Self)

The individual at this mixed level lives both beneficial values and dysfunctional values. The individual may claim constructive values but lives them inconsistently. Actual lived values are often incongruent with professed beliefs. Blind spots about claimed beliefs are apparent, as is resistance to changing irrational harmful beliefs. However, there is a possibility to effect change if initiated by the individual and sufficient reasoning ability is evident.

Level 4: Value Structure (Meta-Self)

The individual's personal values are conscious, congruent, clear, constructive, and lived. There is awareness that values must and will change with new life experience and new learning. This individual is also able to see the values actually displayed by others and compare them to professed values.

Level 5: Value Structure (Meta-Self)

At this highest level of functioning, values are the result of consciously held and lived principles. Values are consistently lived and are objectively and rationally applied in all areas of life. All values reflect and agree with a foundation of constructive principles on which they are created. There is also an understanding of the subtle nature of value application dictated by circumstances.

Element #5: Achievement

Definition: Personal attitude and orientation in regard to achievement and the individual's success at reaching his individual potential for achievement.

Level 1: Achievement (Primitive-Self)

For this individual motivation for productiveness and achievement is absent, with the exception of immediate action for self-gain. Constructive short-term or long-term personal goals do not exist. No history of long-term goals or achievements are evident. A stagnant present and a self-destructive path for future is evident.

Level 2: Achievement (Primitive-Self)

Individual focus at Level 2 is limited to survival or the status quo. Goals for achievement are superficial and immediate. There is no long-range view or plan in any domain of life. An absent or inconsistent work ethic is evident. Underachievement is the lifestyle. Laziness and procrastination with underlying unconscious fear are this individual's primary motivators.

Level 3: Achievement (Mixed Primitive- and Meta-Self)

Motivation for achievement may be present but lacks focus and direction. Goal setting is immediate or vague, and self-accountability is inconsistent. New achievement is minimal. Ability to make decisions is a problem, along with procrastination and a dependence on others for confirmation and direction.

Level 4: Achievement (Meta-Self)

At Level 4 the individual is a well-motivated self-starter with a clear record of productivity and achievement. Programs for achievement are realistic, challenging, well planned, and implemented with confidence. This individual trusts in his ability to make important decisions and holds himself accountable for achieving goals. Achievement may not be evident in all areas of life.

Level 5: Achievement (Meta-Self)

At this highest level, achievement is evident in multiple areas of life, especially in the area of his chosen career. This individual demonstrates consistent achievement and therefore has high credibility in helping others to have higher expectations for themselves and to maximize their personal potential.

Element #6: Power

Definition: Type and quality of power displayed. Methods of influencing others.

Level 1: Power (Primitive-Self)

Power comes through aggression, manipulation, or coercion. Helplessness, suffering, and aggression are primary methods employed to control others.

Level 2: Power (Primitive-Self)

The Level 2 individual is motivated by chronic fear and characterized by his powerlessness in life. Often the individual functioning at this level is used and abused by others as a lifestyle. As in Level 1, he may also be a pathological manipulator of others, primarily employing helplessness and suffering to avoid taking responsibility for himself. Open aggressiveness or passive aggressiveness may also be employed to manipulate or exact revenge on others. Finally, the futile practice of being critical of others to feel better about his self is common. This behavior is coupled with being afraid to stand up for himself honestly to others.

Level 3: Power (Mixed Primitive- and Meta-Self)

Depending on temperament, this individual's power is nonexistent or situational. The individual may have "position" power at work but be powerless in relationships outside of the work setting. He relies on established formal rules in controlled settings to assert power.

Level 4: Power (Meta-Self)

At this higher level, power is based on *personal power* that is a result of a positive self-concept and interpersonal competence, with courage as the underlying motivating characteristic. This individual's power is evident in any setting, professional or private. His has people power — the power to influence others by being real and confident about one's self because of consistently demonstrated competence.

Level 5: Power (Meta-Self)

At this highest level of personal power, the individual displays confidence, courage, and high-level interpersonal skills. He is respected as a person by everyone, including adversaries. He uses his interpersonal abilities to encourage others and hold them account-able. *This power is evident in all areas of his life and in all relationships.*

Element #7: Initiative

Definition: Orientation to taking constructive action interpersonally and in personal achievement.

Level 1: Initiative (Primitive-Self)

The individual at this lowest level is either an isolator who is controlled by fear, or he initiates aggressively with others to intimidate. Constructive action occurs only when forced or controlled by an outside agency.

Level 2: Initiative (Primitive-Self)

This level is characterized by laziness and excuses for procrastination. He might initiate when immediate self-gain is possible and no work or risk taking is needed. Interpersonal assertiveness is absent. Fear of failure and lack of a work ethic are present.

Level 3: Initiative (Mixed Primitive- and Meta-Self)

This individual will act when given encouragement and direction. Assertive ability is evident unless emotionally stressed or high emotional risk is evident. However, initiating new challenges is avoided.

Level 4: Initiative (Meta-Self)

An individual who functions at this higher level is constructively proactive with little need for outside direction. He makes decisions independently, identifies clear and realistic goals, and sees them through. He is assertive but is so while concurrently displaying respect and compassion for others. He will often function better when stressed because of his ability to increase focus and his underlying self-confidence.

Level 5: Initiative (Meta-Self)

The individual at this highest level develops new abstract concepts and new goals and develops programs to achieve them. These abilities are evident in high achievement in many areas of the individual's life. The individual is aware of the underlying methods that led to success in his achievements and knows how to give direction to others when requested.

11

Intrapersonal and Interpersonal Process Conditions

Levels of internal and interpersonal functioning and externally communicated cognitive and emotional quality

The internal and external process condition elements are characteristics that are essential to establishing and maintaining functional and fulfilling relationships, first with one's self, and then with others.

Elements of *intra*personal character are reflected in the course of relating with others. These traits affect the level that an individual is able to display in interpersonal process conditions. These conditions are evident and communicated, to some degree, in every human interaction. We are seen as present or absent, helpful or harmful, caring or uncaring, according to an individual's ability to communicate the conditions. These interpersonal process conditions include genuineness, respect, concreteness, and empathy.

The process conditions must be communicated (exhibited in behavior) to be effective. Simply thinking or feeling them internally is not sufficient. Additionally, the presence or absence of these process conditions is evident in both verbal and nonverbal levels of communication. The recognition of the quality of conditions communicated can be either conscious or subconscious to varying degrees by all parties.

Interpersonal Process Conditions
Levels of Interpersonal Functioning & Communicated Emotional Quality*

Chart #3

Characteristics (Observed interpersonally)	Level 1: Primitive	Level 2: Primitive	Level 3: Mixed	Level 4: Meta	Level 5: Meta
Genuineness Realness and congruence	Perceived as superficial, phony, or lying	Words, emotions, and actions contradictory and inconsistent	Perceived as mostly real; generally consistent and not usually self-contradictory	Consistently real and congruent; honest and direct—even when emotionally stressed	Consistent, congruent across all levels of communication; concrete self-expression
Respect Self-respect and respect for others	Minimal respect displayed; sees others as object for self-gain; no self-respect	Some self-respect evident; superficially respectful to others; focused on self-gain or avoiding conflict	Consistent self-respect and respect for others if no stress or value blind spots are triggered.	High, valid, and consistent self-respect; maintains respect for all during stress or conflict	Respect for self and others displayed and communicated at highest level
Concreteness Economy, logic, and clarity of verbal expression	Illogical, irrelevant, or verbose	Vague, superficial, or intellectually abstract; black-and-white thinking	Expresses own thoughts and feelings clearly and logically when not stressed or when blind spots not triggered	Reflects thoughts and feelings of self and others clearly and logically, even under stress	High level of logical and clear self-expression; clarifies concepts and personal meaning additively for self and others
Empathy Understanding and communication of personal meaning of experience about self and others	Focused on own superficial thoughts and feelings and/or disconnected from self; no awareness of or interest in experience of others	Limited awareness of real self thoughts and feelings; superficial focus on experience of others and used mostly for self-gain	Inconsistent introspective connection to real selfevident; able to understand and respond to the experience of others at basic level	Consistently understands and reflects meaning about self and others; often able to add to others' knowledge of self or experience	Sustained additive responding to experience and meaning; for self and others, isolates common and dominant themes; provides direction and accurate assessment

*Interpersonal conditions are communicated at both verbal and nonverbal levels whenever two or more people are in one another's presence. These conditions communicate the speaker's personal attitude toward others and his own character and are predictive indicators of interpersonal competency.

Element #1: Genuineness

Definition: Realness and congruence communicated interpersonally across verbal and nonverbal dimensions.

Level 1: Genuineness (Primitive-Self)

At this lowest level of functioning, individuals are generally perceived as being superficial, phony, preoccupied, or deceitful.

Level 2: Genuineness (Primitive-Self)

At this level, words, emotions displayed, and actions display incongruity. The individual may say something verbally but negate it nonverbally through voice tone or poor eye contact. Eye contact may also be inappropriate. Interest level displayed is low. The individual may appear distracted or just fail to listen.

Level 3: Genuineness (Mixed Primitive- and Meta-Self)

The Level 3 individual is perceived as real. He is generally saying what he thinks and feels. Verbal and nonverbal levels of communication match. However, when under emotional stress, he may display Level 2 characteristics.

Level 4: Genuineness (Meta-Self)

At this higher level of functioning, the individual is consistently real and congruent across verbal and nonverbal dimensions. He is honest and direct when emotionally stressed. He has the capacity to be appropriately ingenuine as well as knowing when to be genuine. The individual is aware of how his verbal and nonverbal communication is perceived and has control over what he communicates to others.

Level 5: Genuineness (Meta-Self)

At this highest level, all the characteristics of Level 4 are present. In addition, the individual has the ability to read people's verbal and nonverbal behavior and meaning at more profound levels. Internally, he relies on a strong faith in himself to display the courage to be real in all situations and the discriminatory ability to know when and at what level of genuineness to communicate.

Element #2: Respect

Definition: Awareness and degree of respect demonstrated about one's self and demonstrated respect for others. There are three types of respect assessed between people, consciously or subconsciously, depending on the level of mental health and interpersonal functioning of each individual.

Respect is present or absent for:

- the beliefs, attitude, and lifestyle perceived about the other person;

- the amount and validity of the respect the other person displays and communicates about himself; and

- the presence or absence and perceived genuineness of respect communicated back from the other person.

These three types of respect are always being communicated, regardless of conscious awareness of either party. Higher level functioning people, Levels 4 and 5, are more consciously aware of the respect present between individuals.

Level 1: Respect (Primitive-Self)

At this lowest level, the *passive* individual demonstrates little if any self-respect. He may have a history of being dominated and abused in relationships. This individual may also work hard to please others to gain self-confirmation, but he is unaware of his motives and never believes their positive perceptions of him. Inside, subconsciously, his negative self-concept negates all positive feedback.

At the other extreme, the *aggressive* individual is loud and boastful about how much he values himself and is obviously mistaken about it. In reality, he possesses a very low opinion of himself and makes an abundance of noise to convince himself and others of his value. This individual will also have and communicate no respect for others, with the exception of those who believe, or pretend to believe, how great he is.

Level 2: Respect (Primitive-Self)

Some shaky self-respect may be evident in this individual. Interpersonally, he will attempt to communicate acceptance and respect to others out of fear. Actual self-respect is low, superficial, and ingenuine. This individual is other-focused because others define his value on a moment-to-moment basis. Consequently, his internal focus is on pleasing others, to an extreme. His intentions are on self-gain or avoiding conflict with others. He may view himself incorrectly as better than others who do not match his superficial and biased perceptions.

Level 3: Respect (Mixed Primitive- and Meta-Self)

This individual consistently displays self-respect. Respect for most others is genuine but is marred by blind spots or open prejudice. Disrespect may be for people who are different, have different lifestyles, intellectual attainments or deficits, different beliefs, or are of differing racial heritage. These individuals may or may not deny disrespect of others.

Level 4: Respect (Meta-Self)

At this level, the individual possesses high-level and valid self-respect. He will communicate respect to others based on the genuine belief that all persons are of equal value. This belief, attitude, and outward behavior remain intact under stress. Other people are judged on their character, values, and behavior.

Level 5: Respect (Meta-Self)

At this highest level, the characteristics of Level 4 are enhanced by the ability to assess others for their level of self-respect and their ability to communicate genuine respect for others.

Element #3: Concreteness

Definition: Economy, clarity, honesty, and congruence of communication. Concreteness is both an internal thinking element and an ability communicated verbally with others.

Level 1: Concreteness (Primitive-Self)

At the lowest level of concreteness, both internally and interpersonally, thinking and verbalizations are confusing, illogical, contradictory, irrational, and/or dishonest. Projected attitude is fear of exposure or aggressiveness. These individuals are perceived by others as confusing and not trustworthy. Their aggressiveness is without empathy and evokes anger or fear in others.

Level 2: Concreteness (Primitive-Self)

The individual at this level is characteristically vague, scattered, and superficial in thinking and verbalizing. Concrete-sounding opinions reflect biased and all-or-nothing thinking and lack supporting logic and facts. His opinions are often vague, emotionally generated, and unsubstantiated.

Level 3: Concreteness (Mixed Primitive- and Meta-Self)

The individual is able to clearly and concisely express thoughts and feelings if not under emotional stress. Logical thinking is present but at a basic level and inconsistent. His feelings and personal biases come to the surface under stressful conditions.

Level 4: Concreteness (Meta-Self)

An individual at this advanced level expresses thought and feelings clearly and logically. He is also able to clarify the thoughts and feelings of others. His logical thinking abilities enable the understanding and communication of more abstract and complicated concepts.

Level 5: Concreteness (Meta-Self)

In addition to the attributes of Level 4, at this highest level, the individual thinks and communicates clearly and logically in all settings. Ideas are well thought out and supported by all relevant facts. Communications are concise, focused, and additive to the understanding of others.

Element #4: Empathy

Definition: Empathy is a skill. It is the objective discrimination and communication skill comprised of being able to understand the meaning of an individual's immediate or past experience and the ability to communicate that understanding to the frame of reference and satisfaction of that individual. At advanced levels of empathic skill, the responder is able to be consistently additive to another individual's understanding of himself.

Level 1: Empathy (Primitive-Self)

At this lowest level of functioning, empathy is nonexistent. The individual is not empathically connected to himself or others. Focus is on immediate self-gratification without regard for the rights, desires, or needs of others.

Level 2: Empathy (Primitive-Self)

A Level 2 individual has a limited awareness of his real self, with little or no empathic connection to his own true thoughts and feelings. His awareness of his deepest beliefs, particularly about himself, is absent. His empathic understanding of others is limited to superficial expressions of sympathy. An empathic connection with others is absent because it never had a chance to develop. In its place is an inordinate and primarily negative internal focus on his self.

Level 3: Empathy (Mixed Primitive- and Meta-Self)

This individual has a partial introspective connection to his real self. His understanding of himself and others is limited because of blind spots where his primitive thinking dominates. Limited expression of affective empathy is possible in situations that do not trigger his deeper unresolved issues. Emotional stress may cause regression to Level 2 functioning.

Level 4: Empathy (Meta-Self)

At this level the individual is able to respond to content, feeling, and meaning expressed by another person, even if he has not experienced the particular circumstances expressed by that person. Additionally, he has the ability to intermittently be additive to the other individual's understanding of himself. His empathic ability is maintained under conditions of emotional stress, such as in situations where conflict is present.

Level 5: Empathy (Meta-Self)

At this highest level of empathic ability, the individual has the skill to consistently respond at an interchangeable level and at higher additive levels. Observation and discrimination skills are present at advanced levels. Through identifying common and dominant themes observed in the responding process, this individual is also able to isolate deficits in thinking and behavior. Subsequently, the responder is able to provide others additive insight, based on his own experience and acquired knowledge, to increase self-understanding and create goals to resolve issues and deficits. All of these empathic skills are accomplished with genuineness, respect, and appropriate levels of concreteness. This individual is also able to apply these skills internally to facilitate his own psychological growth.

12

Intrapersonal and Interpersonal Competencies

Intrapersonal and interpersonal competencies are human relations skills that stem from and reflect the quality of an individual's character traits and the degree of his interpersonal development. Internal cognitive competencies include rational thinking ability and the quality of the resulting content. External interpersonal competencies are exhibited as social relationship skills. All of these competencies represent the individual's mastery of relating effectiveness, psychologically within himself and outwardly with others.

Element #1: Discrimination Skills

Definition: Discrimination skills are the cognitive skills of reading (seeing) other people. It is reading both verbal and observable non-verbal communications. Discrimination skill is the ability to read feelings, expressed and not expressed, understand personal meaning, and identify the intent or purpose of behavior being displayed.

Level 1: Discrimination Skills (Primitive-Self)

At this lowest level of discrimination, there are two extremes. The first is an individual so self-focused that everything is about him. He does not see others unless forced or strongly encouraged to focus away from himself.

Psychological/Interpersonal Competencies
Levels of Intrapersonal/Interpersonal Functioning & Experienced Emotional Quality*

Competencies (Intrapersonal–Interpersonal)	Level 1: Primitive	Level 2: Primitive	Level 3: Mixed	Level 4: Meta	Level 5: Meta
Discrimination People-reading and understanding skills	Little or none; valued only for self-gain	Some awareness of obvious behaviors; self-centered in interpreting; psychological boundary between self and others weak	Ability to read general behavior; self-focused if stressed; difficulty in understanding meaning and generalizing to behavior	Observant and perceptive of feeling; sees patterns in behavior meaning identifies dominant themes	Able to differentiate subtle behavior—omissions, thinking, and response patterns; acumen in objective concept formation about subjective experience
Listening Objective ability to listen	Hears only what fits own frame of reference or immediate needs	Selective listener; partial hearing if not threatened, preoccupied, or distracted	Listens adequately if own emotions or blind spots are not triggered	Listens objectively; able to put aside own emotions and opinions	Hears unspoken thoughts, themes, and self-perceptions of others; objectively perceptive; hears implied and omitted content and meaning
Responding Verbal responding ability (empathy)	Unresponsive to others; unaware or uninterested: self-focused	Focused on self-interest; manipulative; some ability to respond to others if in emotional agreement	Responds well to general feelings and content; limited meaning comprehension	Consistently communicates understanding to others; responds additively to meaning	Identifies common and dominant themes; isolates real needs, problems, and deficits; provides direction

Competencies (Intrapersonal–Interpersonal)	Level 1: Primitive	Level 2: Primitive	Level 3: Mixed	Level 4: Meta	Level 5: Meta
Relationship Ability to foster, develop, and maintain positive and fulfilling relationships	Focus on short-term self-gratification; takes from others; destructive to relationships	Partially responsive to others for personal gain; relates superficially; not always genuine	Relations mostly positive but limited to people with similar views; loses objectivity when strong emotions present	Wide variety of functional relationships; ability to self-assert with respect when in disagreement; takes responsibility when wrong	Displays broad range of public and private people skills; relates with consistent integrity, congruence, and respect
Program Development Ability to foster and complete programs for self-growth and personal achievement	Absence of focus on future goals; denial of personal deficits; focus on immediate needs	Some focus on needed goals but little ability to conceptualize program or manage self; often fails	Establishes goals and programs in areas of low emotional content; needs direction and encouragement	Establishes goals and programs for self and others; independent and successful self-starter	Comprehensive understanding of program development, implementation, evaluation; teaches all process and concepts to others

*Competencies are both internal (applied to self) and external (applied in relationships). Competencies are reflective of personal character and the degree of the interpersonal process conditions communicated.

The second type is an unethical self-centered individual that can read other people's emotions and needs well enough to manipulate them for his own advantage. This individual's lack of ethics is harmful to others, but he is unconcerned about any damage he does to them.

Level 2: Discrimination Skills (Primitive-Self)

The Level 2 individual has some limited awareness of the meaning of others' behavior. However, typically, this individual projects his own feelings and reasons onto the other individual without being aware of it. Everything the other person says or does reminds him of himself. Another type of individual may have the skill to manipulate others by creating emotional indebtedness.

Level 3: Discrimination Skills (Mixed Primitive- and Meta-Self)

At this level the individual has the ability to read superficial feelings in others and may have a basic knowledge of the causes of those feelings. However, information about himself that triggers internal deficits of his self is ignored. Under stress there is a reversion to Level 2 self-focus.

Level 4: Discrimination Skills (Meta-Self)

At this advanced level of discrimination ability, the individual is able to consistently read the meaning or intent of others' behavior and has sufficient objectivity to read his own. This is a consistent skill that is maintained under most stressful conditions. This individual is also perceptive of meaning beyond the expressed awareness of the other person.

Level 5: Discrimination Skills (Meta-Self)

At this highest level, the individual is able to discriminate deeper meaning in subtle behaviors. He is aware of meaning that is not expressed or consciously known by the other person. He can objectively see and identify response patterns and read psychological intent. At this level, the individual can hear what a person is thinking and what he is thinking at deeper levels that he is unaware of.

Element #2: Listening

Definition: Listening is the level of objective ability to listen to others, as well as your level of ability to objectively hear and own your own internal thoughts.

Level 1: Listening Skills (Primitive-Self)

At the lowest level, individuals hear only their own superficial self-centered thoughts. Hearing others is incidental and only occurs when their own thoughts or feelings are triggered.

Level 2: Listening Skills (Primitive-Self)

The Level 2 individual is a selective listener. This individual attempts to listen *when he wants to,* usually only when self-gain is possible or when the other person is supportive of what he thinks. People who do not agree are discounted. Internally, his cognitive and emotional focus is on himself. Listening to others is feigned to have an audience for his own story or to obtain confirmation or reassurance about his experience or opinion.

Level 3: Listening Skills (Mixed Primitive- and Meta-Self)

At this level an individual is able to listen to others and hear their perception, if not emotionally stressed or threatened. Emotional blind spots about sensitive issues cause regression to Level 2 behavior.

Level 4: Listening Skills (Meta-Self)

At this advanced level, the listener is able to suspend his own frame of reference and objectively concentrate on other people. His own feelings and thoughts are temporarily put aside, and his focus is on hearing the other person's experience. Additionally, he is able to verbally communicate that he heard the other person's message and meaning. Objective listening continues under emotional stress.

Level 5: Listening Skills (Meta-Self)

In addition to Level 4 skills, a listener at this highest level is able to discern unspoken thoughts and feelings, including implied or omitted content. He can also intuit the other person's level of awareness of his own thinking.

Element #3: Responding Skills

Definition: The depth and quality of empathic interchangeable and additive responding.

Level 1: Responding Skills (Primitive-Self)

At this lowest level, the individual is unresponsive to others. Because of his extreme self-focus, he is either uninterested or unaware of the experience of others.

Level 2: Responding Skills (Primitive-Self)

The responders at Level 2 are primarily focused on self-interest. This individual will respond adequately to those who are in agreement. Superficial responding to manipulate for self-gain is evident. At this level, feeling recognition is absent.

Level 3: Responding Skills (Mixed Primitive- and Meta-Self)

The Level 3 responder is able to reply adequately to openly expressed feeling and content of others. Comprehension of subjective meaning is limited. When placed under stress, there is a regression to self-focus.

Level 4: Responding Skills (Meta-Self)

A Level 4 individual is able to respond accurately and consistently, displaying understanding of the other's experience from his perception. He is able to suspend his own frame of reference and avoid contamination of his empathic responding. Additionally, he also has the ability to respond at additive levels to the meaning and experience of others.

Level 5: Responding Skills (Meta-Self)

At this highest level, the individual adds to the Level 4 skills. This individual is able to hear and communicate common and dominant themes evident in the experience that they are unaware of themselves. Furthermore, he is able to identify deeper issues, accurately isolate and specify the real problems, and formulate concrete solutions to problems once they have been identified.

Element #4: Relationship Skills

Definition: The ability to develop and maintain positive, nourishing, and fulfilling relationships.

Level 1: Relationship Skills (Primitive-Self)

Relationships at this lowest level are characterized by either their destructive nature or the absence of any positive connection. This individual is a user of others. In a personal relationship, the person is always harmful to others and a taker, never a giver. He is never at fault and constantly blames others instead of taking any responsibility.

Level 2: Relationship Skills (Primitive-Self)

At this level the individual is able to form relationships but with self-gain always at the forefront of intent. Manipulation of others is a common theme. Common forms of pathological manipulation include the use of helplessness, suffering, and aggression to influence and control others. In the worst cases, all three are employed.

Level 3: Relationship Skills (Mixed Primitive and Meta-Self)

The Level 3 individual generally relates adequately with others that are similar to him in belief structure and place in society. Relationships are often absent of genuineness and intimacy. Nourishing relationships may exist with those who function at the same level. Regression to lower functioning is evident under stress and when crises occur.

Level 4: Relationship Skills (Meta-Self)

This level is marked by the ability to establish a broad variety of successful relationships. Also present is the ability to self-assert in relationships when it is necessary to defend or obtain equal rights. A strong positive self-concept enables him to be assertive in relationships and express expectations to others. Also present is the ability to take responsibility when wrong and the ability to generate solutions to relationship problems.

Level 5: Relationship Skills (Meta-Self)

Relationship skills at this highest level include all of those listed in Level 4. In addition, this individual maintains a highly developed internal relationship with himself. Self-confidence, self-efficacy, self-advocacy, and self-esteem are at the highest levels. Relating to both self and others is accomplished with relative ease in any setting because of his knowledge and competent use of interpersonal skills. The individual believes in his interpersonal ability and the personal power he brings to any interaction.

Element #5: Program Development Skills

Definition: The ability to create and effectively carry out programs for self-growth, personal achievement, and interpersonal relating.

Level 1: Program Development Skills (Primitive-Self)

This lowest level of functioning is characterized by an absence of focus on future goals preceded by the denial of personal deficits. The major focus for this individual is on the gratification of immediate needs.

Level 2: Program Development Skills (Primitive-Self)

The Level 2 individual displays some focus on goals, but the ability to conceptualize needed programs is absent. The individual is either helpless and dependent on others and/or he is a procrastinator, knowing what is necessary for constructive change but always finding a way to rationalize inaction or begin a half-hearted effort and fail. Procrastination is a lifestyle.

Level 3: Program Development Skills (Mixed Primitive- and Meta-Self)

At Level 3 the individual is able to establish basic goals and develop programs in areas of low emotional content. Outside direction and encouragement are often needed to ensure achievement of specified goals. Basic skills and objectivity will falter when the individual is under stress. Blind spots about the self are often evident and become impediments to reasoned thinking and deficit and goal identification.

Level 4: Program Development Skills (Meta-Self)

A person functioning at Level 4 has a history of successfully establishing personal and professional goals and planning effective programs to achieve them. His observed record of achieving goals often elicits help requests from others who need knowledge and direction. This individual has above-average objectivity and is a responsible self-starter.

Level 5: Program Development Skills (Meta-Self)

At this highest level, the individual has an advanced understanding of program development, human behavior, and program evaluation. He is proficient in teaching all program development process skills and the concepts that underlie successful program development and completion. His advanced knowledge and skill set are effective in a variety to professional and personal settings.

13

Man's Misplaced Faith

And ye shall know the truth, and the truth shall make you free.
(John 8:32)

My goal is to teach people how to have faith in themselves and to strive to build a world in which we can all have faith.

Belief in any ethos as a substitute for believing in one's self is always detrimental to one's mental health.

Traditional Religion: A Hypocritical, Psychologically Limiting, and Destructive Ethos

The elements common to all religions are: belief or faith in the unknowable, admission of ignorance, submission of self to an outside authority or higher power, acceptance of contradictory and irrational facts as truth, hypocrisy, and learned fear.

Although we are taught differently, morality and religion are not mutually inclusive. Morality has its origins in man's history far preceding man's creation of religion. Research into the origins of morality traced its roots to prehistoric times when humans began living in groups. Accepted findings among researchers into its origins concluded that morality stems from man's inherent characteristics of reciprocity (fairness), and empathy (compassion). These characteristics are accepted in the scientific community as the basis of morality.[1] Man's current sense of morality has evolved from these basic psychological traits that have nothing to do with religion. The religions of the world would have people believe otherwise.

It is the view of religionists that man must choose between religion and a way of life that is focused only on instinctual needs and material comfort. They view the soul as the province of religion and that to reject religion is to reject the soul. It is my position that the soul is not the sole province of the church, and in fact religion as a whole has failed to nourish man's soul. Religion has never succeeded in molding man's character according to its stated ideals. But what it has succeeded in doing is teaching man that in order to gain the belief of being loved and protected by a higher power, he must submit to required rituals, obedience to authority, monetary contribution, veneration, and the rejection of reasoned thinking. Man must sacrifice his psychological independence, learning to think for himself, and submit, or his lack of compliance constitutes the commission of sin and its well-known consequences.

At their core, religions teach putting one's faith and life in the hands of someone other than one's self and subjugating one's self to their doctrines and authority. This type of believer may be described as the truly devout—they believe the word is *The Word*. Another larger group of "believers" interpret dogma and *The Word* in a manner that better fits their desires. These are the hypocrites who profess one thing and do another.

Yet another more abundant group of believers do as they wish without regard to their professed beliefs, and just rationalize (lie) to themselves about their transgressions and live with their guilt. Every church authority knows that guilt is a great control mechanism, so there are avenues provided for the individual to receive absolution. Asking to be saved by Jesus (repeatedly) or going to confession are two examples. The last type of believer, the most prevalent, are those that believe in, or pretend to believe in, a supreme being—*just in case it's true*. These individuals are also hypocrites.

Being a hypocrite, being submissive to authority, being

---

1 Frans de Waal, *The Age of Empathy* (New York: Harmony Books, 2009).

ignorant—are all characteristics of the religious. Intelligent people hypocritically pretend to believe, just in case it's true, and to be accepted socially. Another integral form of religious hypocrisy is that "believers" are able to commit any sin or crime and receive forgiveness upon request. Thus, any person, regardless of their ethics or morality, can be, or claim to be, religious and be accepted by other believers and ultimately ascend to heaven. Additionally, being religious is often feigned as an effective means to the acquisition of destructive power and influence over others. Fraud is perpetrated continually on gullible believers by those who pretend to be religious and claim to be emissaries of God.

But, people claim, to have religious faith is to have something that provides answers we all need, and if nothing else, provides us with *hope* for an uncertain future—a difficult concept to oppose, right? Being religious also promises that being faithful promises eternal life. And while alive, being an active follower means that people will never be alone. Someone will always care. A belief structure filled with self-deception and false promises.

My grandmother used to say, "Hope in one hand and spit in the other and see which one gets full faster." The truth is, everyone is going to die and no one knows what comes next. We are all alone. We have the genuine love of ourselves and others to buffer that aloneness. If a person values himself and treats himself and others with respect and kindness, he will most likely create relationships in which he is cared for *in this world*. It's up to the individual to construct a personal world that is nourishing and fulfilling.

Man created hell when he created religion. This fact is both literally and figuratively true. Literally, hell is where nonbelievers spend eternity. The concept of eternity in hell is meant to instill fear in the unfaithful. In reality, people have to believe in something before it can evoke fear. Therefore, only believers fear hell or the wrath of heaven.

By the creation of religion, man has created his own psychological prison. Religions are mythical, incongruent, hypocritical, and largely destructive belief systems that are underpinned with psychological fear of the unknown. Man's only solution to his predicament as a believer is to ignore reality and reasoning, renounce faith in himself, and believe or pretend to believe in an external self-support object riddled with unsupported contradictory facts and outright lies.

An individual's early religious indoctrination, and fear of rejecting its tenets, impedes the development of an individual's ability to identify truth about religion and his ability to know truth in general. Reasoned thinking about religion is considered a sin. The individual is taught to accept what he is told to believe instead of learning to discern truth for himself. Psychological growth is limited for anyone that has been taught not to value truth and especially not to use his own mind to identify it. The faithful are threatened with eternal damnation if they choose to search for meaning in their lives outside of the confines of religious ideology.

To my way of thinking, individual man's meaning and purpose, which enhance psychological quality in life, must be created by the individual—not by external authority, doctrine, or the acceptance of traditional beliefs. Reasoned thinking supported by the courage to be an individual is the only effective methodology for discovering truth. Individual man must learn to create meaning and purpose that is identified through reasoned thinking, and the conscious formation of ethical principles that provide guidelines for psychological nourishment and continued psychological growth throughout life.

Man's True Need: Faith in Himself

> *There is nothing wrong with the concept of faith in and of its self—*
> *it is always the object of faith that is in need of questioning.*

Man's faith in himself or in anything else can be rational or irrational, valid or invalid, and beneficial or destructive. Erich Fromm explored the concepts of rational and irrational faith in *Man for Himself*.[2] Fromm concluded man's faith is an attitude and a character trait that he can channel in productive or nonproductive ways.

---

2   Erich Fromm, *Man for Himself*, (New York: Fawcett World Library, 1947), 200.

Man, by nature, is a believer because he is driven by his particular form of higher consciousness to find meaning in both his existence and his eventual demise. The only questions are *what* man is going to believe in and whether his faith is well founded. Man must have faith in something. The absence of faith in something is an expression of profound sadness, confusion, and despair.[3]

If man is to be mentally healthy, and fulfilled in life, he must firstly develop faith in himself. An individual may attempt to develop faith in some entity outside himself, but its success in nurturing him depends on his faith in himself being established first. An individual who lacks faith in himself and trust in his own mind's abilities and does not believe in his value as a person is doomed to a lifetime of suffering, discouragement, and self-defeat. The subjective experience of psychological quality—health, happiness, and fulfillment— depends on the content and quality of his belief in himself.

To date, man has not learned to value his own psychological health. Instead, he has used his creative abilities to fashion myths to assuage his fears. Throughout history, man has created beliefs with the purpose of understanding and justifying his existence and to buffer his mind against the fearful reality of his mortality. Historically, man's chosen beliefs in response to this fear are not only unsound—they are psychologically destructive. Most egregious among man's unsound ideas are his religion-based, learned negative beliefs about his nature and the mistaken mythical solutions he has created to solve these erroneous beliefs.

Religions school man from early childhood about his innate depravity and sinful nature. He learns early that in order to be "healthy" and saved from himself, he must distrust his own mind, seek absolution, and acknowledge his allegiance to a myriad of unsound mythical beliefs. The major result of man's real or feigned belief in the tenets of religion is that it has cost him his belief in both his innate goodness and his ability to value and trust his own mind to determine truth. He is left with the goal of mere survival as a sinner in this life, who hopes (prays) for the best after he dies.

---

3   Erich Fromm.

To the extent man fails to develop a primary faith in himself and the competent use of his mind, he continues to pay the psychological cost of diminished quality as a human being by impeding his own psychological development. Because of the lack of faith in himself and his failure to take responsibility for the substance and quality of his beliefs, he has wrought upon himself an immense amount of needless suffering and in turn has perpetrated vast amounts of destructiveness upon his fellow man.

My central professional goal is to teach people how to have faith in themselves and to focus on creating quality within themselves and with others, in this world. Many times over the years, I have contemplated the idea of undertaking the development of an institute for philosophical and psychological education. In my musings, I call it "The Brotherhood of Reasoning and Love" or "The Institute for the Advancement of Reality, Reasoning, and Responsibility." My purpose for undertaking such an endeavor would be the same as my reason for writing this book. My goals are to teach people how to have faith in themselves in *this world* and to teach the importance of valuing and loving themselves before they can possibly love others in any mature and healthful way. An additional goal would be to teach the value of contributing to the welfare of others as a way of nourishing one's own self. My final goal would be to teach the value of thinking governed by reasoning: Using one's mind to know truth and to teach that one must live truth in order to be able to teach it to others.

It is my fervent belief that human beings are born with an inherent disposition to be good and have the desire to experience the goodness in others. Goodness is used here in the sense that each person is born without a negative perception of himself and the world. Negativity of any kind is learned early in one's life. As I have maintained throughout this book, it is the responsibility of the child's primary caregivers to set the child's course in life. They must value and nurture a child's innate goodness and instill self-value and love. It is belief in one's goodness and value as a person that forms the psychological base for the creation of a positive sense of self and everything else to follow that is beneficial and fulfilling.

Man's goodness is most evident in his need, desire, and ability to love and to be loved. Experiencing being loved as a child provides the necessary psychological underpinning for the ability to love others. Simply stated, goodness, experienced as a positive self-concept, begins with the ability to love oneself and believing that one is lovable. The individual who feels worthy of being loved because he has learned to value himself enjoys the belief in his own goodness and is able to see goodness in others. Any doctrine that teaches man that he cannot and should not have faith in himself and use his inherent abilities is destructive to his psychological well-being.

Rational faith, as defined by the philosopher Erich Fromm, is the result of conscious productive experience and reasoning in which man uses his inherent human capabilities to their fullest extent to know and live truth.[4] Man must actively pursue (live) what he values in order to have faith in himself. His chosen values must be based on a knowledge of and respect for objective reality. Man can only develop faith in concepts of love, reason, equality, or justice by consciously experiencing them. If they are absent from conscious experience, their value and even their existence is lost. To be truly believed, values must be known and lived.

Rational faith is the productive blending of reality, reason, and experience. It begins with the development of faith in one's self through the *experience of love and reason*. Through the experience of love and reason in unison, one gains confidence in one's worthiness of love, ability to love, and in one's ability to observe and think clearly and objectively make valid judgments.

Rational faith—believing in one's self and one's capabilities—enables an individual to develop faith (trust) in others. The more confident one is in his ability to make good judgments based on sound reasoning, the better his judgments about self and others can be. The formation of faith in one's self and others lays the psychological groundwork for the ability to have faith in the potential of humankind to build societies based on the principles of love, reason, equality, and justice.[5]

---

4   Erich Fromm.
5   Erich Fromm, *The Sane Society* (New York: Fawcett Publications, 1955).

Faith is a concept that has meaning that transcends its definition within a narrow religious context. Faith is an example of *subjective truth*. It is a subjective psychological entity, a belief ascribed about an object. One can have faith in anything or anyone. *However, having faith or belief in anything or anyone does not prove the veracity of that belief.* In other words, having faith does not justify the existence of its object. We may believe there is life on other planets, but that belief does not prove their existence. Many believe that god exists, but that does not make it true. Right, it doesn't make it false either. The truth is, we do not know.

For faith in anything to be valid, its veracity must be evaluated through reasoned thinking to verify in logical fact or actual objective reality. Additionally, if we are to validate a belief, its beneficial worth must be established and then compared to any harm it might cause. Blind faith, in any entity, without demonstrated beneficial validity and value is the province and product of the ignorant. "God works in mysterious ways that are beyond our understanding" is just one example that says, "Just accept what religious authorities say, don't think independently, trust in the judgement of others who know more."

To believe in and to have faith in love as a concept is an example of a reasoned valid belief. Its value and beneficiality can be seen in human interaction in countless ways. Problems will arise in the course of loving or because of the poor choice of the object one chooses to love. These reality events have nothing to do with the belief in the concept of love as a beneficial entity.

Faith is a necessary and beneficial trait if formed and applied with reasoned thinking. The most critical form of faith with regard to mental health is faith in one's self. I know the value of one's self as an object of faith, both personally and professionally. Faith in one's self is an absolute necessity for establishing and sustaining mental health. Most mental health problems, disorders, "diseases," can be traced to underlying problems with one's self-concept.

Belief in any ethos as a substitute for believing in one's self and directing one's own life is detrimental to mental health. In this world, which by the way is the one we all live in, it is vital to establishing mentally healthy character and promoting constructive psychological growth that the individual develops faith in himself. *Believing (having faith) in one's self is the basis of mental health.*

Mental health is not substituting faith in one's self with pledging blind faith to the tenants of any external authority or ethos, be it religious or otherwise, just because it is professed and adhered to by many. The idea that mental health or truth should be found by conforming to the beliefs of the majority is both absurd and a fertile foundation for the development of mental illness. Oftentimes the majority of people are wrong. Accepting the irrationality of others as truth leads to further irrationality. *Mental health lies in the quality of the individual's judgment—his faith in his own mind to know truth—and to actually live it.*

I do believe that once a person has a healthy self-concept and faith in himself and his mind's ability to know truth, he is then ready to answer larger questions about life. He is able to establish humanistic principles and values that are beneficial to himself and all of mankind. Those principles and values must grow out of the fundamental concepts of love and reason in order to be supportive of man's psychological health. Such humanistic principles must then be lived instead of worshiped.

Major Tenets of Rational Faith

- There is nothing wrong with the concept of faith in and of itself—it is always the object of faith that is in need of questioning.

- Any doctrine that teaches man that he cannot and should not have faith in himself and use his inherent abilities is destructive to his well-being.

- It is belief in one's goodness and value as a person that forms the psychological base for the creation of a positive sense of self and everything else to follow that is beneficial and fulfilling.

164

- Believing (having faith) in one's self is the basis of mental health.

- The soul is, after all, individual man's subjective beliefs about himself, his purpose, and the meaning of his life.

- Rational faith—believing in one's self and one's capabilities—enables an individual to develop faith (trust) in others.

- Mental health lies in the quality of the individual's judgment—his faith in his own mind to know truth—and to actually live it.

- The hallmark of psychological maturity is when an individual achieves conscious rational faith in his ability to constructively manage his own thoughts, emotions, and actions.

As I spoke about earlier, psychology has continually abdicated its role of providing insight and ethical direction in man's life. Instead, subjects such as morality, love, reasoning, and values are avoided even though they are elements of man's soul.[6] It is the province of psychology and philosophy to provide the content and direction that is beneficial and congruent with the better parts of man's nature. The soul is, after all, individual man's subjective beliefs about himself, his purpose, and the meaning of his life. He needs to know what is good and bad, right or wrong, and how he could live his psychological life being healthier and able to experience a more fulfilled life. These are rational goals for *this* world.[7]

---

6   Erich Fromm, *Psychoanalysis and Religion*, (New Haven, CT: Yale University Press, 1950).
7   Ibid., 35.

14

Developing a Mentally Healthy Adult Meta-Self

The Personal Challenge of Positive Self-Change

Real, beneficial, and enduring self-change begins with acceptance of the psychological three R's as new life values. No, they are not "Readin', 'Ritin, and 'Rithmetic." Rather, I'm referring to the three R's for psychological health and fulfillment—*reality, reasoning, and responsibility*. These elements are the essence of the three fundamental meta-principles.

Changing one's self for the better is difficult because it requires both a strong personal desire and the psychological and intellectual abilities to challenge who one is and sustain positive growth toward who one wants and needs to be. Initially, change requires a person to have the courage to be open to seeing and owning his real self and also have a willingness to consider new knowledge that challenges the veracity of his current beliefs.

One last obstacle that challenges the individual's desire and ability to change is the presence of fear as the primary motivator for everything he does or does not do. Fear is deeply ingrained in individuals who possess a negative self-concept. An individual may be consciously aware of his fear, or it may be repressed deeply in his subconscious mind. An individual who lives motivated by fear spends a lot of energy avoiding the conscious experience of his fear. However, the more fear is denied or repressed into the subconscious, the more it dominates the thinking and actions of an individual.

One of the first actions an individual seeking positive change must be able to do is to summon courage as his new motivator in life. It takes courage to begin and sustain self-change; therefore, one of the first new constructive meta-self principles that an individual must adopt is: "I will continually identify my fears and challenge them." This is true especially when confronting the fear of knowing the truth about one's self.

Fear is a powerful motivator because it is learned early in life, and therefore it is an integral element of one's *primitive-self*. Regardless of chronological age, individuals with a dominant primitive-self have a propensity for allowing fear to undermine their change efforts. Temporary regression to the comfort and safety of the primitive status quo, even if it is painful, is part of the change process. Familiar pain is more acceptable because it is predictable. The unknown is not. Because of the presence of fear as a major element of a negative self-concept, building the meta-self is therefore always two steps forward and one step backward.

Individuals who have doubts about their need to make changes in the quality of their self-concept might consider some of the following questions:

- Do you feel good about the real you?

- Is courage your primary motivator in all that you think and do?

- Do you constantly create distractions to avoid time alone with yourself?

- Are you connected to your real feelings and thoughts about yourself?

- Do you feel like you are more than one person inside?

- Is your mind constantly at odds with itself?

- Do you experience unresolvable inner conflict about too many things?

- Do you trust your mind to know truth and make sound decisions?

- Are you able to make and maintain fulfilling relationships?

- Is your behavior in relationships destructive?

- Do you make your own judgments about yourself instead of letting others judge you?

- Is your life on a good psychological path for the future?

- Do you display your real self to others?

- Does the emotional age you feel match your chronological age?

- Are you a person worth being loved?

- Do you believe you are valuable—as a person?

If an individual's answers to these questions are honest and troubling, it may be an indication of a disturbed and divided self—a self that is, at a minimum, psychologically underdeveloped, and possibly psychologically and interpersonally impaired.

If the individual can accept that at least part of the problem is within himself, he will have achieved the first step in really changing the quality of his life. Accepting responsibility for being the cause of his problems means he is willing to see his real self. He is *ready to begin identifying and owning what he does and does not value about himself.* He is prepared to know and evaluate the validity, functionality, and overall quality of his current beliefs about himself and the world. He is ready to begin the journey toward increasing the quality of his experience of himself, his experience with others, and with life in general.

The Psychological Costs of a Negative Self-Concept

Improving the quality of one's psychological life is a challenging endeavor because it demands that the person change much of what he now believes to be true about himself. Who he learned to be—what he learned in early life as truth about himself and what was therefore possible for him in the world—is ingrained in the deepest levels of his mind. Those early learned beliefs are hardwired in one's being, one's definition of existence. Once established they control the person's destiny—*even if they are destructive to him.*

Early learned beliefs form the individual's perception of reality, and once in place, everything observed is filtered through that perceptual window. The individual's early learned beliefs influence every decision made in life. To be beneficial, these beliefs must not deny actual reality, be harmful to him, or limit his psychological development as a human being. Healthful early learned beliefs enable one to make rational and constructive sense out of the experience of one's self and the outside world. They give the individual direction toward achieving all that life has to offer. They allow him to develop psychologically toward becoming a mentally sound and mature adult.

When beliefs about one's self or the world are negative, healthy psychological development is adversely affected. The ability to feel good about one's self and meet the challenges presented by life diminishes with each passing year. Failures mount and discouragement grows. Successive external solutions are attempted to change the experience of life for the better, but nothing really works. Over time, a negative attitude and behavior becomes increasingly harmful to self and others. Thoughts and feelings become more negative and confused, yet the individual denies or represses the real truth about himself. Eventually all attempts to deny or escape from reality will fail.

Too often, the solution to a negative self-concept is to deny its existence and to find an escape in destructive behaviors that only complicate the problem. To escape from troubled thoughts and behavior, people use alcohol, medications, emotional and physical isolation, dysfunctional relationships, overeating, overworking, or other addictive and destructive behaviors. *Their underlying goal for their destructive behaviors is always the same—to escape from their real selves.*

The prevalence of drugs, both legal and illegal, and even the failure of the national "war against drugs" are persuasive evidence of the many self-medicating millions who are unhappy with their lives. These external solutions may provide temporary relief, but they also make life increasingly worse for the individual and for all those who relate with him. If these self-defeating thoughts and behaviors progress too far, they cannot be reversed. The individual is destined for self-destruction.

Many other troubled individuals who are not as obvious as those with addictions are people who are constantly negative about themselves and/or others. Being chronically negative about one's self or others is a destructive lifestyle based on conscious or subconscious irrational beliefs. What are the irrational beliefs held by critical people? Everyone has their own, but here are a couple of common examples: At a subconscious level one might believe, "Being negative and critical about others proves to me and others that I am a better person." Or, at a conscious level, "I'm just a person who tells the truth, and people don't like it."

Thinking or talking negatively to an excessive level about others is actually a learned way of attempting to feel better about one's self by making others appear worse. However, being excessively critical does not really work to make anyone feel better about who they are. If it did, they would be happier people. In reality, being excessively critical only provides surface relief as a temporary distraction or escape from the reality of a troubled self. With time, being critical alienates the negative person from others. Given enough time, the individual will also become consciously disgusted with himself. No one can escape forever from one's real self. Neither can a person escape the eventual consequences of negative harmful thinking and behavior.

Last, but not least, is the effect of a negative self-concept on building trust in one's mind to know truth. A negative mind denies the value of truth and reasoning. It accepts only what agrees with it in the moment—with its current reality. An individual who thinks negatively does not see his contradictory thinking or his flexibility with what is true at any given moment. Because a negative mind constructs conflicting truths and/or avoids truth to suit its immediate needs, it can never know real truth. Consequently, an irrational negative mind cannot trust its own thinking processes. At the subconscious core, a person with a mind that cannot be trusted to know truth lives in fear—the fear of not knowing. *Fear, conscious and subconscious, becomes the primary motivator for all thinking, feeling, and action.*

At the worst levels of dysfunction, a person motivated by fear is not consciously aware of their fear. Fear resides deep in their minds at a subconscious level, and most of their mental energy is spent avoiding anything that would put them in touch with the conscious experience of it. At a lesser degree of impairment, where individuals are aware of being afraid, considerable energy is spent avoiding situations and subjects that could invoke fear. Fear as a primary motivator is a debilitating and destructive force over the course of life. Its existence is a significant sign of a divided trouble self. People who have fear as their primary motivator cover it with anger or isolation, depending on their temperament.

The Self-Help Process of Becoming a Psychologically Healthy Adult

Whether an individual is a professionally trained helper or a member of the general public, the process of taking responsibility for one's level of mental health and interpersonal functioning is the same. Initially the individual must be healthy enough to know that there is something wrong with him. If he is able to see and own the need to change himself, then he is ready to face the biggest challenge of his life—changing who he is.

His next challenge is to overcome the natural and deeply ingrained resistance to change. A person's present primitive-self will view change as loss of self-identity and existence and will resist. It will let an individual try anything, but it will undermine any efforts in order to survive in its primitive state.

Resistance to change is a constant throughout the transformation process. The person must be both determined to change and patient with himself. Progress during the psychological change process is always two steps forward and one backward. Regression is going to happen; do not let it discourage you. Every person who attempts psychological change in their lives faces this challenge.

Successful psychological change is not an easy process. *Therefore, an individual may or may not be able to succeed without outside help.* His level of mental soundness and reasoning ability will be the determining factor in his decision to help himself or seek objective outside assistance. If the individual does not function at Level 3.5 or above in most of the elements, then he probably is going to need outside professional help. This minimum level of healthy functioning is especially critical in the elements of self-concept, reality base, and reasoning ability. By the way, the accuracy of a person's self-rating depends on his objectivity and honesty with himself about his level of functioning on the various elements. To increase objectivity, an individual might ask someone that they consider equal to or above their perceived level of mental health and interpersonal competency to rate them.

Additionally, an individual could consider another avenue to assess his need for change. In my book, *My Enemy—Myself,* I have provided a means for the reader to identify and specify at the deepest level how he or she feels and thinks about themselves. Some will be able to use this guide on their own successfully, while many others will need guided professional help to achieve the process of knowing and accepting who they really are by learning their true beliefs about themselves. The goal of *My Enemy—Myself* is to help individuals identify core beliefs about their selves. This information is critical in the change process because people cannot change what they cannot see or have not accepted as truth about themselves.

People who have reached adulthood with a negative self-concept have also learned, as a psychological survival mechanism, to minimize or disconnect entirely from the knowledge of their real beliefs about themselves. The goal of this first stage of self-change is to become aware of the beliefs, perhaps formed many years before, that are still causing the individual to have a negative perception of himself in the present. Uncovering negative self beliefs gives an individual the opportunity to evaluate their validity. Are they rational or irrational? Are they beneficial or harmful? Do they help or hinder him in his relations with others? Do they enhance his experience of himself? Once identified, his core negative beliefs can be replaced with beliefs that are valid, reality bound, and beneficial.

To disconnect from beliefs necessitates disconnecting from feeling. Not feeling provides the necessary insulation from self-awareness and the conscious experience of psychological pain. Therefore, the first step in the change process is the reconnection to feelings. This can be a difficult process, depending on the degree of disconnection established by the individual.

Awareness of feelings and *actually experiencing* them is a necessary first step because of their role as the doorway to knowing one's real self. Once the individual has begun to reconnect with feeling, he must also learn to identify the specific reasons for each feeling. Identifying the thoughts that generate feelings leads the individual toward conscious realization of his core beliefs.

The process of connecting to feelings and reasons requires both patience and persistence because psychological resistance to change is always present. An individual who has been disconnected from his feelings for a long time will find it difficult to reconnect because in disconnecting from negative feelings, the individual had to sacrifice connection with *all* feelings. Reconnection to feelings and the thinking that created or caused those feelings is a gradual process requiring patience and determination. The length of time needed will be determined by the individual's present level of psychological impairment.

Building a Positive and Functional Meta-Self

Building the *meta-self* begins with the process of reconnecting to feelings and the thoughts that preceded them. That process was not initiated by one's primitive-self because it does not want change. To the primitive-self, change would mean loss of control and potential destruction. *The process of reconnecting with the real self is initiated by and managed by the meta-self.*

Although in the beginning an individual's meta-self may be undeveloped and weak, it is there in the mind awaiting the necessary conditions for its emergence. As a direct response to the incorporation of Meta-Value #1, Seek and Live Functional Truth, the meta-self has begun the task of reconnecting the individual to his real self. The individual has begun to identify and conform to what is real and true instead of believing out of habit. The meta-self's new role is to identify and accept objective or subjective truth that is functional and beneficial. Its role is also to identify and reject thinking that is invalid and irrational. To accomplish this goal, the meta-self must challenge all previous beliefs, especially the ones learned in early childhood. To achieve this lofty task, the meta-self must begin to learn and invoke reasoned thinking. Reasoned thinking (Meta-Value #2) must be employed because it is the only way to identify functional truth and provide constructive direction.

The process of building a functional meta-self that is able to assert its constructive control over the individual's mind is a gradual, deliberate process. As the meta-self develops and strengthens through the above described mental process, the individual is increasingly able to discern the difference between negative thinking that is created and controlled by the primitive-self and thinking that is controlled by the meta-self. Learning to discriminate which portion of the mind is at work is a critical part of developing the meta-self's dominance as the mind's default thinking entity.

Gradually the individual will learn to choose the thinking of the meta-self because of the functional positive results that occur. With time the primitive-self's control will be diminished. As the meta-self gains positive control, one of its primary functions will be to assume the role of a mentally healthy parent to the individual's primitive-self. In other words, the individual is going to assume the role of parent to his childhood self. This relationship should be one in which the individual's meta-self becomes the responsible, empathic entity that interrupts negative thinking, positively reframes it, and provides understanding and positive direction. The individual's constructive parenting of himself is a necessary substitute for the less-than-adequate parenting received in the formative years. By learning to self-parent, the individual is concurrently establishing his meta-self's dominance as a responsible and mentally healthy adult.

Meta-Self Principles for Mental Health

A major part of building and maintaining one's meta-self, healthy adult self, is the conscious development of principles. These psychological principles become the conscious guidelines needed by all individuals who wish to develop and maintain mental health and interpersonal competency.

Although each individual must be responsible for building conscious principles to guide their life, it is my belief that everyone's individual principles must begin with the acceptance of the three fundamental meta-principles. *All other functional and beneficial principles and values are corollaries of the three meta-principles.*

Meta-Principal #1: Seek, know, and live functional subjective truth—reality.

To live truth is to live one's life as a process of seeking and living in reality. It is through the experience and acceptance of reality supported by reasoning that man discovers truth. Living truth is also seeking the reality of true self-knowledge and objective knowledge about the world. It is also living consciously in the present—in the here and now.

Meta-Principal #2: Live life guided by conscious, reasoned thinking.

To live with reason as a value is to practice conscious and constructive thinking (reasoning) as a way of life. Reasoning is the logical and unbiased pursuit of knowledge and understanding focusing on the identification of truth—the essence of things and processes.

Meta-Principal #3: Seek, know, and live a lifestyle of psychological growth.

Valuing psychological self-development entails fostering and maintaining a lifestyle of responsible psychological growth. In other words, psychological growth is the means to realizing psychological quality, and it is predicated on living the first two meta-values.

Individual Meta-Self Principles as Lived Values

Building a set of principles is a personal undertaking. Meta-self principles are found by the individual observing his conceptual and overt behavior and then exploring the thinking that caused the behavior. Each individual must identify the beliefs that motivate his surface thinking, feeling, and behavior and evaluate those beliefs for validity and positive functionality. Beliefs that do not contribute to the individual's life in some positive constructive manner must be discarded and replaced. The process of consciously identifying and writing principles promotes understanding and ownership of one's efforts.

By the way, the concept of forming and living by principles is already a part of our lives. It's just that most of us are unaware of how they were formed, or their content. We all have principles, rules that we live by, for better or worse. At their most basic level, principles are our beliefs that we consciously or unconsciously follow. These beliefs were created early in life by the individual in response to his environment. These personal beliefs become principles that define subjective reality and direct the course and quality of life. What's important is the validity of the principles followed, and if valid, are they actually adhered to, or only professed? Principles, values, and other beliefs that are not actually lived or only lived part-time do not really exist.

Constructing Meta-Principles

Building meta-principles is a conscious, ordered process that seeks to incorporate and integrate relevant facts that respect reality and identify functional subjective truth. These truths become the foundation of the new principles an individual adopts and lives.

From the perspective of his meta-self, a person learns to hold himself accountable for these actions:

- Objectively observing his thoughts, feelings, and actions. Compiling truth about himself. Substantiating things he believes and values. Developing programs to change those things he does not like.

- Evaluating his thoughts, feelings, and actions for origin (cause), validity, and how and when to appropriately express them.

- Building a library of opinions and concepts he believes in because he has employed reasoned thinking to formulate them as truth.

- Valuing functional beneficial truth over myth, previous learning, tradition, the status quo, and the opinion of authorities.

- Evaluating all beliefs for congruence (noncontradiction). Watching for exceptions to perceived truth. Any given truth may not apply in all cases. Developing justifiable concepts to support his position about these exceptions.

Corollary Examples of Meta-Self Principles

Meta-Self Beliefs about Me:

- I am a person of value.

- I deserve to be treated with respect and kindness.

- I will think and behave only in ways that make me feel good about me.

- My thinking must be independent of the opinions of others. I am the final judge of the quality of my thinking.

Meta-Self Principles about Relating with Myself:

- I must hold myself accountable for living in my meta-self at all times.

- My meta-self must govern all thinking and actions.

- Treat myself with kindness, respect, and empathy. Recognize and value all my positive traits.

- Challenge fear to build courage. Every incident is an opportunity for discovery and growth.

- Do not indulge in negative self-talk. Be self-critical but own deficits and find solutions.

- Be empathic with myself but do not accept excuses for my mistakes.

- I will be my own self-advocate. I deserve to be successful and happy. I will find a way to make it happen.

- Slow my mind down to invoke reasoned thinking—speed means emotions are in charge.

- Thoughts are behaviors that cause emotions—pay attention to their quality.

- Be alert for inconsistencies/incongruence in my thinking and behavior.

- I must be productive and achieve commensurate with my abilities to value who I am.

Meta-Self Principles about Relating with Others:

- I am the judge of my thinking and behavior—not others.

- Every interaction is an opportunity to learn about others and myself.

- Conserve energy by spending it wisely; decide if the expenditure is worth it.

- Be a thinking observer, not a talker. 80 percent observation—20 percent talking.

- Talk to others only if they really are listening. Do not waste energy on those who will not consider any belief other than their own.

- Be open-minded to truth from any source—especially those with whom there is disagreement.

- Give to others and expect/demand the same in return.

- People who cannot or will not reason are only able to hear behavior. Learn to change behavior in a way that they have no choice but to hear.

Meta-Self Principles about Truth and Reality:

- In any specific case, identify functional subjective truth—live it.

- Strive to see all perceptions of any event. Select any salient points from all and form the best truth possible.

Meta-Self Principles about Reasoning:

- Use reasoned thinking to evaluate all thinking and behaving for validity and beneficiality to me.

- Rely on my mind to tell me what is true.

- Have faith in what truth my reasoning finds. Be open to new knowledge that may change it.

- Value reasoning over emotion to identify truth.

- Avoid hasty assumptions, opinions, and generalizations—gather *all* the facts, then formulate and decide.

Meta-Self Principles about Psychological Growth:

- Pursue psychological quality in the present.

- Learn what is mentally healthy and live it.

- Keep meta-self beliefs fluid—open to new learning and truth.

The Meta-Self in Relationships

Individuals who have developed themselves in a healthful psychological manner to the point of being governed by a strong *meta-self* live in relationships differently than others. People who value themselves and are responsive to the rights and needs of others have high expectations of themselves and those with whom they relate. Believing one has the right and the responsibility to have expectations in a relationship and having a clear understanding about what is legitimately needed and desired gives one the confidence to express those rights and expectations and hold others accountable for meeting them. Mentally sound individuals are "givers" in relationships as opposed to being "takers." They have learned a valuable lesson. The more one gives to others, the more they will give in return.

For example, in choosing a mate, you should be clear on the traits and behaviors that are a must for you. You should also know the qualities that you would like to have in a mate but would be willing to compromise on because they are of less importance. Physical attractiveness or beauty may be one of these to consider. Remember, in the long run, the ability to trust and respect someone is more important than physical beauty. However, there is no substitute for chemistry. Attempting to compromise too much and force one's self to focus solely on internal character will not work either.

Experiencing Psychological Quality

Experiencing psychological quality in life is both an immediate goal and a lifelong process of committed growth as a human being. It is a continuous quest for faith in one's self through self-awareness, self-understanding, self-acceptance, and self-directed change. Learning to engage and develop one's meta-self is the only way to accomplish these goals. It is only by building the power of one's healthy adult self that a person will be able to consistently feel good about who he is.

The journey of positive change entails a difficult process of identifying the self-limiting and self-defeating beliefs of one's primitive-self, as seen from the perspective of the meta-self. It requires employing the meta-self's perspective to identify, adopt, and actually live new constructive beliefs as conscious principles for governing all thinking and behavior. Meeting the challenge of positive change also requires an attitude of openness to new learning: a resolve to consider new knowledge and skills and the courage and determination to incorporate the changes that will surely follow.

Principles for Living Psychological Quality

- Identify and accept reality/truth.

- Identify and live the best subjective truth in the moment, given the context. Remember, most of what we call truth is man-made subjective truth. Therefore, any truth is open to reasoned challenge.

- Challenge the fear of disapproval, failure, and deservedness. Develop faith in your mind's ability to discern truth.

- Learn how to think with reasoning. Reasoned thinking is the only way to know the best subjective truth for any given situation. It's the only way to build faith in your mind.

- Always employ reasoned thinking to identify truth, not simply following emotions. Use reasoned thinking to identify truth, clarify thinking, make decisions, and for challenging all that one believes for veracity.

- Reject myth, tradition, authority, majority opinion, etc., unless they can hold up to the scrutiny of reasoned thinking.

- Hold one's self accountable for personal psychological growth. Be responsible physically, intellectually, and psychologically. Being responsible means knowing what is right and doing it. Make learning and growing psychologically a lifestyle.

- Have conscious goals that are to be achieved in all areas of life. In a larger sense, develop a vision of how life should be and develop programs to get there. Have conscious internal goals that are about personal characteristics that are yet to be developed.

- Mentally, constructive self-integration or individuation is one's major goal. This means becoming one person inside and out. It also means not being at odds with one's self. Being one's own best self-advocate. Take conscious responsibility for quality thinking and behaving. Personal responsibility is a core feature of the meta-self.

- Get nourished by creating meaning and purpose in life. Don't depend on others for motivation. It only comes from within. Always be productive and have goals to achieve; they are the major contributors to valuing one's self.

- Be empathetically connected internally and externally with others. Seek reality, reasoning, and responsibility in one's self and in all others. Observe internal thoughts and feelings during interactions with others. Focus on genuineness, respect, understanding, and constructive action.

- Be constructively self-critical and build programs to change or overcome deficits.

- Be a self-advocate while being self-critical. Be honest about mistakes, strengths, and deficits. Recognize attributes and take action to correct deficits.

- Find ways to contribute to the welfare of others. This is the best way to nourish one's self.

- Do things that generate good feelings about one's self, and avoid all that leads to thinking and feeling bad.

- Do not lie. It is impossible to not know it, and it undermines a positive self-concept.

- Experience the pride, self-respect, and general satisfaction about living with psychological quality.

In Summary

The challenge of improving one's self-concept is not an easy task, but if an individual is able to take psychological responsibility/ownership of the fact that the cause of his problems and their solutions are within himself, then real and lasting self-change is possible.

Developing a healthy adult self, a meta-self, is positive self-change toward mental health. Fundamental to this volitional process is Meta-Principle #1, Valuing Truth/Reality. Individuals who seek mental soundness and psychological quality must learn to identify and conform to what is real and true instead of believing what they want to. To accomplish the transition to knowing and living truth, all beliefs, especially the deeply rooted ones acquired in early life, must be challenged for truth. This challenge must be directed by reasoned thinking—the only way to identify truth and provide constructive direction in life. The act of starting this process requires the activation and continued development of one's meta-self, *the responsible overseer of an individual's mental health.*

The meta-self principles presented in this chapter are not meant to be all-inclusive. They are but a representative sample of what is possible. Each individual must develop his own personal principles that give meaning and direction to his life. Remember, we all already have principles in place that determine the course and quality of our lives, for better or worse. It is the sole responsibility of every individual to identify and evaluate his principles for veracity, rationality, and beneficiality.

Conclusion:
Post-Empirical Direction

The Challenge for Psychology: Becoming a Rational, Subjective Science

Carl Rogers, in *A Way of Being*, raised the question of whether psychology would continue to be a narrow technological fragment of science, tied to an outdated philosophical conception of itself, clinging to the security blanket of observable behaviors only, or whether it can possibly become a truly broad and creative science, rooted in subjective vision, open to all aspects of the human condition, worthy of the name of a mature science.[1]

Rogers believed that it is professional psychology's responsibility to be a major force in attacking the society beliefs and issues that are major contributors to mental illness. He stated that psychology needs to stop being a past-oriented remedial technology. Instead, it must take its part in changing a chaotic world by working to build social environments where human beings can choose to learn, where all people, regardless of culture or race, can learn to live cooperatively together. Thus, psychology can be part of the solution to mental

---

1   Carl Rogers, *A Way of Being* (New York: Houghton Mifflin, 1980), 257.

illness by addressing its causes instead of being seen as a group that applies Band-Aids over symptoms.

In conjunction with a major role change, Rogers challenged the field of psychology to improve its treatment effectiveness and, as a corollary, the clinical competence of its practitioners. Rogers emphasized that people who work in the field of psychology should be judged not by the number of certificates and diplomas they have but rather by the *quality of their work and its effectiveness*.[2]

Other research has cited needed changes at the theoretical level, specifically a move away from a traditional empirical model. Hansen (1958)[3], Popper (1955)[4], and Gergen (1991)[5] concluded that effective theorists approach the world with the theoretical position already in place in order to interpret and separate meaningful facts. The theorists must proceed from theory to observation, not the traditional empirical converse. The researchers concluded that *psychological research is not an objective process but rather a subjective social process*.

The arguments presented above were forward-thinking attempts to encourage the field of psychology to evaluate itself at both theoretical and applied levels. Their words call for the field to be more responsible and to adopt a more realistic and effective direction. Their critiques highlight the philosophical division in the field that has persisted for the past fifty years. This philosophical division is yet to be addressed or resolved.

In 1993 I published an article in the *Journal of Psychology* that examines the role society, and psychology as its agent, play in the growing problem of addiction and mental health in general. In that article, I examined the philosophical roots of psychology, its theories and methods, and their mistaken role in perpetuating erroneous beliefs about addiction and ineffective treatment methods.

At the theoretical level, I also criticized the field for limiting itself

---

2   Ibid., 245.
3   N. R. Hanson, *Patterns of Scientific Discovery*, (London: Cambridge University Press, 1958).
4   K. R. Popper, *Conjectures and Refutations: The Growth of Scientific Knowledge*, (New York: Harper & Row, 1956).
5   K. J. Gergen, *Emerging Challenges for Theory and Psychology*. Theory & Psychology, 1 (1991) 13-35.

to the theoretical tenants of traditional empiricism, which assumes the objectivity of the scientist as a researcher. Empiricism and its theoretical assumptions of valuing *only quantitative, objective, scientific perspectives,* and the exclusion of *qualitative, subjective viewpoints,* has led to a polarization of theorists and practitioners within the field of psychology. Psychology has become a collection of diverse theories and methods that are characterized by their lack of demonstrated effectiveness.

Psychology must accept its logical heritage as the leader in finding real solutions to mental health issues. To accomplish this goal, psychology will have to rely more on reasoning rather than assumed objectivity and artificial levels of statistical significance.

The field of psychology must change how it thinks and what it does in order to make the profession more relevant and effective. The profession cannot continue to avoid the subjective arena of man's values, beliefs, and most of all, his perceptions of himself. This book has focused on what I believe is the subjective center of man's existence, his subjective self-concept. If individual man and mankind as a whole are to be mentally healthy and interpersonally fulfilled, then building a positive sense of self is the starting point. Without a positive self-concept, everything in life that is valued and needed by man for his survival and fulfillment as a human being is diminished or destroyed.

The profession also will need a unified and clearly defined common goal, namely the pursuit of mental health. And to that end, it must be courageous enough to risk defining mental health's content in commonsense terms that everyone can understand. Identifying mental illness and treating it, to be successful, has to be predicated on knowing what mental health is. Without this knowledge helpers at all levels of certification and experience are left to provide "treatment" with no direction or standards for success. Currently, instead of having clear standards for defining mental health, the treatment community relies on vague success terms such as "improvement in the quality of life." This is an ambiguous concept that allows any interpretation. Without specifying the characteristics of mental health, the labeling of any particular behavior as mentally healthy or unhealthy is nothing more than arbitrary and capricious.

I join in the challenge to the field of psychology to live the first meta-value, to value and seek subjective and objective truth as a guiding force in their work. This will require mental health professionals to also learn to value and apply the second meta-value of employing reasoned thinking in their quest for truth. I challenge psychology to choose the goal of knowing, living, and teaching mental health as its universal goal.

Of course, to succeed with this direction, it is first necessary for the profession to define the elements of mental health both rationally and practically. I challenge them to clearly define its content and competencies. They must also define mental health at both the individual and societal levels. Following are some of the relevant questions that must be addressed.

In relation to the specification of elements of mental health:

- What character traits and competencies do mentally healthy people possess? How are they acquired?

- What are the mental processing skills of reality-based thinking?

- What are the psychological elements that allow some to achieve psychological adulthood while others are trapped in perpetual childhood?

- How does the psychological quality of parenting affect the development of self-concept?

- What factors enable mentally sound people to feel good about who they are and believe in themselves and their abilities?

- What are the interpersonal abilities that separate competence from dysfunctional behavior?

As the primary agents of psychological education and treatment, professional psychology practitioners must also ask themselves:

- What changes do we need to make in our profession in

training and practice to hold ourselves accountable for our responsibility as leaders in mental health advocacy?

- Where, when, and how do we as professionals proceed to teach the characteristics and competencies of mental health?

In psychology's role as a responsible leader in societal change, the following issues must be addressed:

- What are the societal causes of mental illness?

- How can psychology address these issues to promote real change?

As for assuming the specific responsibilities that come with actual leadership, the profession of psychology must pursue the following:

- Identifying the elements that make an individual mentally healthy. These would include character traits, attitude about self and toward others, and age-appropriate psychological character traits, cognitive abilities, and interpersonal competencies, just to name a few.

- Assuring the mental health and competency of its professional practitioners as well as the wide variety of nonprofessional helpers.

- Identifying and teaching mental health competencies to groups who have a profound effect on the developing mental health of children, such as parents, teachers, and lay counselors.

- Teaching mental health elements and competencies to the public. Using mass media as a means for reaching vast numbers of people.

This book is an initial step toward achieving the goal of identifying the factors that contribute to the development and conservation of mental health and the sustained experience of psychological quality in all of our lives. The elements and characteristics of mental health and interpersonal competency I have presented are valid for both individuals and to mankind as a whole.

The future of those of us living today, and the quality of life for our progeny, will depend on how much we grow psychologically as human beings. I believe that our very survival will depend on raising the level of our mental health and our ability to use the unique gift evolution has given mankind—the capacity to think rationally.

Critique my ideas, and then improve upon them. A person who exercises the right to criticize assumes the responsibility to provide an alternative that is better. If he cannot improve upon it, then his criticisms should be ignored.

Bibliography

Bergin, Allen E., and Sol L. Garfield, 1971, 1980. *Handbook of Psychotherapy and Behavior Change*. New York: John Wiley & Sons, 1971, 1980.

Branden, Nathaniel. 1969. *The Psychology of Self-Esteem*. Los Angeles: Nash Publishing.

Carkhuff, Robert R., and Bernard G. Berenson. 1967. *Beyond Counseling and Therapy*. New York: Holt, Rinehart, and Winston.

Fromm, Erich. 1947. *Man for Himself*. New York: Fawcett World Library.

Fromm, Erich. 1950. *Psychoanalysis and Religion*. New Haven, CT: Yale University Press.

Fromm, Erich. 1955. *The Sane Society*. New York: Fawcett Publications.

Gergen, K. J. 1991. *Emerging Challenges for Theory and Psychology*. Theory & Psychology, 1: 13-35.

Hanson, N. R. 1958. *Patterns of scientific discovery*. London: Cambridge University Press.

Jahoda, Marie. 1958. *Current Concepts of Positive Mental Health*. New York: Basic Books, Inc.

Manwell, Laurie A. et al. 2015. "What Is Mental Health? Evidence Towards a New Definition from a Mixed Methods Multidisciplinary International Survey." *BMJ Open* 5 (6).

Peele, Stanton. 1989. *The Diseasing of America, Addiction Treatment Out of Control*. Toronto, Canada: Lexington Books.

Peikoff, Leonard. 1993. *Objectivism: The Philosophy of Ayn Rand*. New York: Penguin Books.

Popper, K. R. 1956. *Conjectures and Refutations: The Growth of Scientific Knowledge*. New York: Harper & Row.

Rand, Ayn. 1964. *The Virtue of Selfishness*. New York: New American Library.

Truan, C. Franklin. 1993. "Addiction as a Social Construction: A Postempirical View." *Journal of Psychology* 127 (5).

Truan, C. Franklin. 2004. *Meta-Values: Universal Principles for A Sane World*. Tucson, AZ: Fenestra Books.

Truan, C. Franklin. 2014. *My Enemy—Myself: Overcoming Your Self-Defeating Mind*. Tucson, AZ: Wheatmark.

Vaillant, George E. June 2012. "Positive Mental Health: Is There a Cross-Cultural Definition?" *World Psychiatry* 11 (2). https://doi.org/10.1016/j.wpsyc.2012.05.006.

Waal, Frans de. 2009. *The Age of Empathy*. New York: Harmony Books.

Wason, P. C. and P. N. Johnson-Laird. 1972. *Psychology of Reasoning*. London: B. T. Batsford, Ltd., p. 237.